GOD,
WHY DID YOU
DO THAT?

BOOKS BY FREDERICK SONTAG
Published by The Westminster Press

GOD, WHY DID YOU DO THAT?

THE FUTURE OF THEOLOGY:
A Philosophical Basis
for Contemporary Protestant Thought

GOD,
WHY DID YOU
DO THAT?

by
Frederick Sontag

THE WESTMINSTER PRESS
Philadelphia

ISBN 0–664–24886–1

Library of Congress Catalog Card No. 71–114715

Published by The Westminster Press ®
Philadelphia, Pennsylvania

PRINTED IN THE UNITED STATES OF AMERICA

For
G. F. S. T.

O my son Absalom, my son,
my son Absalom!

—II Samuel 18:33.

Contents

Only a personal God can be asked by
the rebel for a personal accounting.

—*Albert Camus, in* The Rebel.

PREFACE

Perhaps for too long now we have treated God too gently. In the face of both the widespread atheism of our time and the church's inner dissensions, the only reasonable direction for us to take may be to try to extract from God a clear and a fresh answer to our crucial questions. The essay that follows attempts to do this, and it arose out of a twin need. First, a series of questions grew in my mind which were addressed to God. Second, while lecturing to a class on the problem of atheism, I discovered that the problem of evil, and our modern techniques for correcting natural defects, combined to form perhaps the most important source of atheism today. Thus, unless God is interrogated along these lines, little is likely to arise to reverse atheism's tide.

During the fall term of 1967–1968 I delivered a series of lectures on atheism to Roman Catholic seminarians at Sant' Anselmo, the Benedictine International College in Rome. In order to discuss atheism, I felt compelled to consider the ancient question of theodicy, and so these chapters were written in order to "answer" the demands of atheism. The students in that seminar read and then were kind enough to prepare criticisms of those lectures. The essay that follows is a much revised version which, I hope,

shows the benefits of the discussions with that class of
critics. Those who are inside the confines of formal religion, I found, do not always take the problem of evil as
seriously as those who are estranged from the church
because of this mysterious injustice. In any case, in the
light of the troubled state of religion today, theodicy demands serious attention once more.

Many authors are taking up the question of evil again,
but this present discussion has, the reader will discover, a
different approach from that of most standard theology.
Perhaps this is because the author is essentially a philosopher and a metaphysician who uses those tools to deal
with theological questions. In any case, as many and as
wide a variety of treatments of evil are demanded today
as can be written.[1]

The slightly unorthodox approach of this essay, it is
hoped, may induce the reader to take a fresh perspective
on an ancient problem. Of course, as one Roman semi-
narian remarked, "Now I see what your God is like and
I don't care for him!" In any new encounter with God, this
reaction can be expected, since he is perhaps the most un-
settling being whom man can meet. Yet, the question still
remains: Has anything true been uncovered as a result of
our proposed divine confrontation?

All those who made possible that extraordinary year in
Rome have been mentioned in other volumes as the various lectures of that year appear in print. I will not thank
each person individually again, even though I should. It
is hard to imagine how this essay could first have been
written except in the midst of those unusual circumstances
in a Roman Benedictine monastery and with a secular philosopher confronted by that very different student body.
Mrs. Gloria DeLia typed the rough draft for lecture distri-

bution and then the revised manuscript, both with amazing conscientiousness. Mrs. Barbara Benton once again helped put the draft into final form.

The Waldensian Seminary in Rome kindly bound the text of the original lectures for deposit in their library. Anyone who compared that first draft with this final version would guess how many changes have taken place in those first rough ideas. Evil does not allow itself to be treated easily and without a struggle.

He to whom this little volume is dedicated has heard its question addressed to him many times in love. Time alone, plus affection, will tell whether he has learned an answer.

F. S.

Claremont, California

Chapter 1

A LOST AND FOUND FOR GODS

As the reader progresses through the succeeding chapters, he may come to think that some particular theory of the divine nature is being assumed and that it either is not made clear or its derivation is not explicitly defended. That is both true and not true. As will be mentioned shortly, an exploration of the sources of atheism in our time did lead to the formation of a new concept of God (to be explained briefly below). However, where evil is concerned, we do not usually start with a concept of God and emerge from the problem with the same God intact. Some ideas of God are bound to be lost when the force of evil overwhelms us.

On the other hand, whether or not our old idea of God survives an encounter with the problem of evil, a new concept of God can be forged under the pressure of those fires. Job certainly understands more about God at the end of his testing than he did during his days of happiness, that is, provided that he does not yield up his God under the pressure from his comforters. Evil, rather than sunny days, may be the best circumstances in which to find a God, although he is not likely to be exactly the same God as the one we originally lost. We often need an inducement to make us think about God, and evil sometimes supplies that force. Unfortunately, sometimes it does so in super-abundance. Facing the problem of evil can be "a lost and found for Gods." This is a situation in which an easy concept of God is likely to slip away but where it is also possible to gain a new insight into the depths of the divine nature.

As the concept of God employed in this essay becomes clear to any reader, he may ask: Did you choose this conception of God to work with first, or did facing the problem of evil bring you to this conception as a means to provide an answer? The reply, of course, is neither completely on one side nor on the other. Ordinarily we do not just happen to start thinking about God. Something must drive us to do this, since there are many easier things to do in this world, e.g., simply enjoy life. In this case, a facing of the problem of the evil which is present in creation raised the issue of God and started my search for a conception of God new enough to deal with that problem more easily and successfully. However, once you are forced to this point, you do not begin completely fresh; rather, you start to call up and to test the classical views of God and the solutions to the problem of evil which follow from them.[2]

In this sense, a classical notion of God forms the starting point for this essay but, as the reader will discover, not its conclusion. That is, as we face the radicalness of the problem of evil in its contemporary statement, the original concept of God must be modified to meet it, so that the God who emerges is not in any usual way "classical." Of course, he may be in the sense that no concept of God can be entirely contemporary. The idea of God arrived at here actually must contain classical components from many sources, although certain features of the God who emerges may be given a novel stress, e.g., will. To admit that I began with a "classical" notion of God would be more determinative of the outcome if in fact there were only one such concept. However, a major premise of this essay is that we always face a variety of concepts when we think about God, whether these are drawn from the past or from the present.

What circumstances lead us to think about God? In this case, it is a reflection on the kinds of choices which God had to make in creating the world. The assumption is that God's choice was not fixed and determined, that he had more than one option and combination of factors to choose from. The choices that God made which lie behind the created natural order should form the background against which the problem of theodicy is considered. Our question becomes: In what way can we think of God as acting both rationally and out of a motive of love and at the same time choosing our world with its excessive suffering, injustice, and wrong? In an attempt to answer this query, one of the solutions to be considered is whether God might use excessive evil to express excessive love.

Underlying the whole consideration of God must be the acceptance of that element of will in God by means of which he acted in ways that do not fit reason's standards as we know them. Yet, so the argument goes, these actions are justified insofar as we can understand God's freedom to create just the kind of world in which we find ourselves. In order to understand both evil and God's actions, then, we need to understand "will" almost more than "reason," although each is involved in any divine decision. In some cases, reason alone may be sufficient to provide the needed

explanation. If so, evil is not included. If not, "will" becomes the crucial faculty whose operations must be
fathomed.

As the reader proceeds, he will become aware that,
gradually, certain important aspects of a new idea of God
have been introduced. What may not be quite clear is why
certain assumptions are made and where the various notions about God come from. However, this indirection and
these omissions are intentional. The assumption is that,
peculiarly in this case, God is best understood by not
focusing on him first. Instead, the way we have to proceed
is to introduce such assumptions about him as seem required in order to deal with the question regarding both
his intentions and the presence of evil.

In this sense the criteria used must be "pragmatic." You
cannot simply construct an ideal model of God, but first
you must deal with a very pressing personal problem, i.e.,
evil. Under this pressure, you are forced to introduce such
notions about God as seem to fit the practical facts being
accounted for. Of course, the various ideas about God do
not come out of the immediate facts themselves. They
come from the accumulated tradition about how God has
been and can be thought about.[3] Then these various notions are applied to the present facts whose brutality forced
us to test our original idea of God.[4] First we consider the
problem of evil, and then our idea of God can be modified
in the light of this and in response to our need for an
answer.

As the argument proceeds, the reader may also wonder
to whom the author is addressing his remarks. Of course,
as the title indicates, the first person under question is
God himself, because we learn more about his nature when

we discover how God responds to our interrogation concerning his action in creation. The style adopted is not the usual mode for theological discussion, and yet this is a serious treatment of a central theological issue even if it is gone about in an unorthodox way. The question is also addressed to any reader, not just to Christian theologians, since all men face the problem of evil. Anyone interested in religion must learn to think about God in this light or else eventually lose all sense of divinity.

In the strictest sense, this treatment of God does not aim to take sides (at least not just yet) on many of the serious problems regarding the divine nature. Hopefully, a more technical treatment of God can be built on the discoveries introduced here, but to do that is not the intent of this brief essay. "Substance" vs. "process" as a way of thinking about God, for instance, is a serious matter, but for the moment we can sidestep that issue and face the question of evil first. In doing this, we certainly hope that giving attention to a concrete and pressing problem may in fact provide the necessary material and context upon which more technical issues can later be decided.

In another essay[5] I have attempted to uncover the philosophical roots for the widespread atheism of our time, and then, using this as a basis, to construct a concept of God capable of resisting those forces. That was a philosophical attempt, whether or not every philosopher would recognize it as such or pursue it in that way. Philosophy's first job is always to define itself, its method and its procedures.[6] The original investigation of atheism, and the kind of God that those arguments suggest, is philosophically based, i.e., no conscious appeal is made to any other source and every line of reasoning is open to philosophical appraisal.

Nothing prevents the resulting theory from having a theological or religious use; in fact, the hope is that it will actually find such employment.

In contrast, this present effort is an essay in theodicy, and, as such, it rests on slightly different ground. Philosophy has pure modes, but it also has mixed modes, i.e., in its relation to science, politics, religion, etc., and both phases are important to it. Theodicy is always a "mixed philosophical mode." It begins from a philosophically constructed concept of God based on the arguments for atheism (see below for a brief account of this) and then adds both theological and religious interests. Can the view of God's nature constructed here yield a new answer to the traditional questions of theodicy, i.e., the attempt to justify God's ways toward man? It is important to any concept of God to see whether it can. However, in order to do this, that concept must be placed within a particular theological orientation and put together with more specific religious materials.

In considering atheism, I suggest that its primary roots lie in the problem of evil and in our conceptual failure to construct a God who reflects contemporary concerns, i.e., a God about whom we can speak directly and against whom we can work out specific answers. If a concept of God can actually be formed by such an analysis, the problem of evil will still not be directly answered. If we attempt to do that now, the discussion will necessarily begin to have a basis other than philosophy. This is because the question of evil (at least in Christian terms) always involves a reference to the future. Philosophy, in testing its arguments, may appeal to the future, but more commonly it tests itself against either present analysis or accumulated experience. If the answer to theodicy unavoidably involves reference to a future which is said to be radically different in structure from the present, then a tentative philosophy will become even more uncertain as to the degree of validity which it dares to claim.

On theological or religious grounds, one may accept this appeal to the future. It may even be important for theodicy, as it is not for philosophy, to allow this orientation toward a changed future to be accomplished by radical divine intervention. Philosophy may be future-oriented too, if it has a logic of dialectical development and if it extends forward the patterns that it discovers.[7] Any religious appeal to the future is of an order different from this; it involves an intercession on God's part which cannot be predicted simply on the basis of the past or the present. As is sometimes claimed, God may have "revealed" his intentions in this regard, but no revelation can be such as to compel universal belief. Moreover, in the case of Christianity any revelation is subject to a certain variety of interpretation. To take the materials of revelation and the religious tradition and attempt to mold them systematically in order to answer theological questions is a valid effort, but it is a different kind of enterprise from what follows here.

If a philosopher can develop a concept of God, then within the structure of the divine attributes as outlined he should next attempt to "speak of God," i.e., to employ his concept to see how it responds when problems are raised. If the question concerns evil and its future solution, the philosopher is merely a philosopher insofar as he develops his concept of the divine nature further. However, if he moves on to predict future changes not presently visible, then he is employing that concept of God religiously, and his mode of philosophy is no longer pure but mixed. He is not dealing with strictly empirical materials; he is using a concept of God in order to predict changes not discernible from the physical structure itself. As philosophers have learned by experience, to enter into a practical realm, whether it be politics or religion, is an intrusion that does not always bring thanks to the philosopher. Practical men, whether politicians or priests, have never been certain that they needed philosophy; and, to be sure, for their immediate success they may be better off without launching into such a questioning of basic assumptions as philosophy demands.

To put the point in the mode which this essay assumes: To interrogate God is the philosopher's proper business, but only insofar as he works in metaphysics and has formed a concept of God. As any idea of God becomes clearer, the traditional questions about God's actions also appear, and the shape which the answers will take should be outlined by the concept of God. That much is philosophical, i.e., to form the questions and to limit the range of answers that are possible. This essay will do that much, but it will also do more. It will attempt a specific answer, and in doing this we are essentially "speaking for God." Yet when this is done we leave the more strictly philosophical context with which we began and move into the area of theology. Now the theologian can decide whether this "divine reply" fits in with his tradition, and the religious man can see whether for him the philosopher has, like Kant, made faith possible once again.

Since God's nature is not obvious in its detail, we actually need the metaphysical structures created by the philosopher. By means of these we can rise to a consideration of God's nature and to a discovery of the reasons for his decisions in creation. When men then offer specific answers based upon this insight, this "speaking for God" becomes a philosophical work as it is applied to the religious situation—and now it is subject to all the weaknesses of a mixed enterprise. However, someone must answer the pressing questions in God's name, and this is the theologian's burden. If he elaborates his replies on a philosophical base, this is not blasphemy, because the metaphysical context for the answers that are given is clearly recognized to be what it is, i.e., of human origin. The attempt to provide this philosophical foundation seems more important today than ever—for reasons which this essay hopes to make clear.

Of course, a Christian might answer that he does not need such help from a philosopher, that God has "spoken" in his revelation. As important as this is, the interesting fact is that any revelation tends to be silent on just these two points: (1) Why God made the world as he did with the degree of evil which we find in it when he might have done it differently, and (2) the details of the structure of God's nature within which alone the answer to such questions can be found.

Whatever it may say for itself, revelation needs supplementation at these crucial points, and philosophy has traditionally provided this assistance. Sometimes such superimposed structure distorts the meaning of revelation, but it need not. Since revelation is never definitive and clear but is indirect enough to require amplification, we have no choice but to seek philosophic assistance if we are to reach an acceptable solution. Revelations speak of a future promise and of a possible present unseen participation in a different life, but human beings first need to understand what God is like and why he made the world as he did. After that they can listen to the promise made in revelation.

Then they may be in a position either to reject it or to hear it and to believe.

There is no question but that, religiously speaking, atheism is the most forceful single factor on the contemporary scene. It might seem that this would exclude God, but what I have suggested is that, if the factors which lead men to atheism are accurately appraised, it is possible to take this evidence and construct the concept of a God who can meet the force of these arguments. This is taking negative evidence and building a positive concept out of it. If this can be done, it most certainly affects the way in which evil is accounted for, since the force of evil itself is one of the most persuasive factors leading to atheism.

From a prior consideration of atheism, certain factors can be deduced about the characteristics of God's nature. However, it is too simple to say that some abstract description of the divine attributes underlies this consideration of evil. Where God is concerned, we face the classical dilemma of "which comes first, the chicken or the egg?" We do not simply begin thinking about divine attributes in the abstract, nor can we deal with any practical problem involving God (e.g., evil) without falling back on some notion of the makeup of the divine nature. Where God is concerned, no issue is unconnected; and we can arrive at a satisfactory conclusion, not from any one consideration alone, but only as our many approaches to God begin to coalesce and to yield a concrete picture.

It is also impossible to list any strict set of questions or absolute procedures that must be followed. If this could be done easily, God would not have been such a difficult philosophical problem for so many centuries. The "logic" needed in order to consider God develops one step at a time, and the problem that forces itself on us initiates our first thoughts about God. The same kind of "pragmatic" approach determines our conclusion or our resting point too. That is, where God is concerned, the issue is never ended conclusively. The issue goes on and God must be rediscovered constantly; we come to a stop only when the material is exhausted and when we have achieved a sense of resolution or climax. That, of course, is neither an absolute point nor a specific stopping place that can be specified, but it contains a built-in individual factor. However, men are not basically unalike and so their response to evil and to God may uncover some agreement among them.

In this present age, the problem of theodicy seems to have changed its complexion, and thus Chapter 2 begins by considering how a "divine scandal" has developed recently. Problems in metaphysics remain fundamentally the same in all ages, but the context within which they are treated can take on novel aspects, and our success in dealing with these (e.g., God) will depend upon our accurate grasp of the novel elements in our own context. Today our attitude toward the necessity of nature has changed under scientific pressure, and we can no longer accept either "necessity" or "goodness" as a reason why God created as he did. Thus, the "divine scandal" comes about because we realize that God deliberately chose the world we experience—including its horrors as well as its virtues—when other better options were available.

If we are tempted to think that the question of theodicy can be approached with neutral terms, Hume teaches us otherwise, and thus Chapter 3 begins by exploring Hume's basic assumptions. By studying Hume's argument, we discover how, in seeking a solution, his philosophical first principles drive him in one direction or another. Therefore, the question of philosophy (or, more precisely, of our metaphysical first principles) is raised at the outset and must be dealt with before we can proceed to theodicy. We might think that first we arrive at a conclusion theologically and only later discover certain compatible philosophical methodologies. Actually, it seems more to be the case that, where God and evil are concerned, we cannot even advance toward a solution until our philosophical first principles have been developed and stated.

If we think that philosophy is the only question we must settle before we can answer the question which this essay asks, Jung (Chapter 4) teaches us that our religious context is equally important and that it must also be scrutinized before we can arrive at an answer. Jung considers Job "in a cold light," and he could not understand the morality of a God who acted that way (i.e., unfairly). What we learn from Job and Jung is that divine action makes sense only when it is set in a religious context. Or rather, in order to understand any report of an action by God, we must first work out an acceptable setting of religious practice within which to interpret it. God does not act alone; the context for his action is always a religious one.

At this point (Chapter 5), we are ready to consider the kind of metaphysical context needed in order to deal with the question of theodicy. The various metaphysical outlooks that we can use are multiple. Therefore, it is important to make clear at the outset the kind of view of the world's structure that forms the setting which will make an answer to this question possible. In no case is the reader required to agree with the author on these three basic frameworks (philosophy, religion, and metaphysics), but we must begin by showing how important our decisions on

these matters are and how they influence the kind of conclusions we can reach.

If God is often lost from sight because of the destructive
force of evil, it is also true that some concept of God
must be recovered or constructed (Chapter 6) or else the
question will remain unanswered. Therefore, the next
question in logical order is to decide which of the possible models open to us we are going to use to think about
God. In questioning the reasons for the extent of evil in
creation, we are dealing with God's actions and not directly
with his nature. In order to answer the question, however,
we must form a picture of his nature in terms of which
the results of his actions make sense. Of course, any concept of God does not grow entirely from observing the
results of his actions but is partly formed from our knowledge of previous descriptions of God.

When we reach Chapter 7 we are finally ready to begin
to answer for God (which is the theologian's task) the
questions we have put to him. In this case, I have chosen
to focus on the question of the divine will. In other answers
to the problem of theodicy, different attributes of God undoubtedly can be stressed: the features you take to be most
characteristic of the divine nature are crucial in shaping
your answer. Given the decisive role of the divine will in
determining the form of creation, we discover what kind
of answer we can expect and just how far it can go toward
being satisfactory. We see God more clearly as the solution
to the question of evil gains clarity, and vice versa.

Since God does not act only for the moment, we cannot
ask about evil without introducing questions about the
future and about long-range outcome (Chapter 8). Somewhere along the line, we must judge whether we consider
the whole drama to be a tragedy or a comedy in its total

perspective. Christianity has announced that the divine intention is to transform a present tragedy into an eventual comedy. As far as the question of evil is concerned, the announcement of God's ultimately happy intent only serves to highlight—not to lessen—the difficult problem of the strong force of evil precisely because its presence is so much opposed to what we are told God intends to bring about. We are left with no choice but to try to understand evil in terms of God's ultimate aims.

When the reader reaches this point in the essay (Chapter 9), it should be abundantly clear that the author is not going to be able to produce an absolutely necessary and unalterable conclusion to this problem. In fact, the drift of the argument points in the opposite direction, i.e., that what we need to learn most of all is to live with less than certain answers (i.e., with probability). This is the first thing which an exploration of the origin of evil accomplishes. The demand for certainty must be broken before the question of theodicy can be answered, and this may have the healthy effect of training us to live with an irreducible and basic uncertainty.

If "freedom" is a major philosophical problem of our day, it certainly turns up as the crucial factor in our questioning of God's actions (Chapter 10). In the first place, we have sometimes been told that opening the world to the intrusion of evil was a necessary consequence of God's choice to give man freedom. Man could not be free without being free to be destructive, so the theory runs. However we may appraise this argument, it is clear that we must arrive at some interpretation of "freedom" before we can account for either God's action in creation or man's subsequent behavior. Where evil is concerned, it still remains a question of just how much man's freedom actually explains and also whether freedom seems to be worth this awful price.

In the Biblical account, of course, the human position is said to be jeopardized, and thus to have been made unfavorable for all men, by an original sin (Chapter 11). Evil's presence cannot be accounted for without considering and perhaps reinterpreting the question of whether man, through his own actions, has placed the entire human race in a position that predisposes all of us to error. Whatever we may decide about the literal historical facts, the issue at stake where human beings are concerned is whether our inherited context does in fact prejudice us toward failure. Perhaps we exist in a situation that makes the odds of our right conduct not as favorable as we might hope.

The Christian claim to have received a revelation of God's nature contains many aspects, but always central to it is a discovery of God's democratic love for all human beings regardless of their condition. At first it may seem that this revelation solves the problem of evil for those who accept its message. In fact, what proves to be true is that such a discovery about God only heightens the tension where the problem of theodicy is concerned (Chapter 12). The all-too-often cold world we live in would seem more natural if it were the product of a God who does not care quite so much; it is clear that evil cannot be understood unless God's "love" can be comprehended. What can love be like and still be compatible with the voluntary inclusion of destructive evil in our world?

The Postscript, which concludes this essay, is not a final chapter, because a definitive conclusion is not available to us. It *is* possible to give some answers; and those which the author gives can be inspected by the reader, but primarily what we can hope to learn is the best way to ask and to phrase the question itself. Only each individual can provide an answer for himself, but the function of philosophy is to provide a clear background for the questions. The job of the theologian is to adopt some set of basic assumptions and to test the various answers which can be given on that basis.

The question of evil and of God's involvement in it is a "lost and found for Gods." Whenever life is smooth, then an idea of God may survive in our minds undisturbed. When destruction and an obvious evil intent open up an abyss before us, then God has more trouble surviving the storm, and he may be lost in the fury. If, however, we can learn to deal with the problem of theodicy again, a new idea of God can be recovered. This is not a promise given to every prospective reader. All the author can guarantee is that, locked in the midst of the question of evil, Gods can be found as well as lost. This may be the only possible answer to the question which the title asks.

Chapter 2

THE DIVINE SCANDAL

In *The Republic,* Plato made a theological advance for his time. He insisted that the gods were to be held accountable, not for everything, but only for the good.[8] He objected to the popular stories that attributed to the Greek gods the same type of objectionable conduct to be found among men. In this way Plato helped to develop the tradition that allows perfection to be attributed only to God, and theology was set in motion for centuries exploring the ways in which God's nature is perfect in contrast to man's.

As long as there were counterforces, as long as there were origins of evil and chaos not under God's control, this development of divine perfection could proceed. However, as a single first principle and creative source came to be preferred to a multiplicity of sources to explain creation, a problem arose as to how to preserve the Platonic tradition of the perfection of God and still account for the origin of imperfections in the created order. The defects in nature became more and more obvious to us, and they seemed to be incompatible with simple perfection in a creator God.

The ways to overcome this difficulty are legend, and the Neoplatonists are the masters at reconciling existing evils with an all-good source. Most of the suggested solutions to this problem of reconciling evil and a good God have involved the acceptance of a metaphysical determinism. Difficult as this consequence was for human freedom, it seemed for centuries to be preferable either to admitting the existence of multiple deities, some of which were malign, or to accepting imperfections into the divine nature itself. Modern man, for all his rebellion against tradition, somehow seemed to accept determinism and never to direct his revolt against this basic principle.

Perhaps the answer is this: If man had received too much freedom, it might have threatened his cherished rationalism, that is, his conviction that every event has a single, rational explanation. Faced with such a choice, the modern philosopher accepted determinism easily. It remained for postmodern man to challenge God's pure perfection in the name of freedom, since freedom is the concept that dominates the twentieth century. If necessary, God's death would have to be announced in order to open the way to human freedom and self-determination in the postmodern era.

The twentieth century uncovered the divine scandal, and it is one that had been suppressed for centuries: God must now be held accountable for absolutely everything, all actions and every feature of the world, not just the good and the pleasant. Faced with such a difficult conclusion, we had the alternative of retreating into atheism, and many men have preferred to do this rather than to hold God freely responsible for willfully creating the multitude of unpleasantness which they witness.

When freedom enters and becomes a major concern, the situation is made both more difficult and also easier. When men are cast out on their own, when their actions are not predestined from eternity, then God has less direct responsibility for each human decision. On the other side, when the world's form is no longer held to be necessary, then we realize that every imperfection which we have finally overcome or corrected by human scientific endeavor could have been eliminated by God at the time of creation. He must have known originally the solutions that we discovered only late in man's history (e.g., anesthetics). Faced with this, we are driven to the conclusion that he purposefully chose to include every horror to which the world exposes man when he might have eliminated any one or all of them had he cared to.

Heidegger has told us that the basic question is: Why is there something rather than nothing at all? Such a question goes partway to the heart of our concern over evil, but it does not drive deep enough. Theists have disagreed about the means employed and the purposes intended, but all have agreed with Plato that what is good tends to communicate itself in production. This tendency to create holds true even if the time, place, and the conditions of its creative action remain indeterminate. The real question, I suggest, is: *Why is the world formed in this way rather than in some other?* We have recently discovered that many deficiencies which we previously accepted can now be corrected. If we can improve upon the system, we assume that God could have too, and we want to know, Why didn't he do so in the first place?

Today no action or structure can simply be accepted without alternative. Prompted by the explosion of scientific knowledge, we are discovering just how many alternatives there are and just how many improvements can be made. Either we will have no God at all, or else we will have one whom we can interrogate constantly and hold responsible for freely choosing every known deficiency. "Why did you do that?" is the question constantly on our lips when we address God in the mid-twentieth century. Such a question exposes the Divine Scandal which has shocked men in our time.

Kierkegaard and Paul each focuses on another and more traditional scandal. The Christian assertion that God became man at a point in time and in a particular person seems, especially to Kierkegaard, to involve both incommensurabilities and an incredulous mode of behavior for a deity. However, what shocks one age usually does not offend another, and we in our time have learned to domesticate infinities and to expand our own grasp seemingly without end. If the Greeks found the Christian doctrine of the incarnation of God scandalous, contemporary man finds nothing so shocking in that now-classic assertion. Of course, a postmodern man may choose not to believe such an announcement at all; but, if he does not, it is no longer simply because such action on God's part is rationally offensive. What is "rational" and what is "irrational" depend upon how one defines reason, and our ways of doing this are now flexible enough to include unions of the finite and the infinite if we care to have them.

Today the divine scandal takes a different form. To every mode and situation we can see alternatives, and many of these are better. We find that there are a multiplicity of value norms and not just one. The given structure of our world does not lack its beauties, but we are sure that its horrors and its terrors need not have been so extreme. What we find scandalous is that God deliberately chose to leave in so many offensive features when he perfectly well might have accomplished the same ends in less destructive ways. Some choices seem to us offensive on the part of a God whose own calculations might have corrected them just as our intelligence now can. What harm would have resulted if hereditary insanity had been programmed out of the biological mechanism from the beginning?

Traditionally God's responsibility for our suffering has sometimes been lightened by making this world's structure the only possible one, so that we are faced with the choice between this world or nothing at all. When he asks, "Why something rather than nothing at all?" Heidegger is traditional in his conclusion, but he is novel in approaching it via the negative side. When we were able to conceive of other possible worlds, Leibniz' view became the standard conclusion: this is the best world possible, given a desire for balance, variety, etc.[9]

However, now we know too much to be satisfied with such a simple answer. In the face of the resulting scandal, some theologians have abandoned theology, i.e., they no longer try to answer these accusations for God, and thousands have preferred atheism—no God to a God who willfully tortures. We can eliminate much illness, move against starvation, and attempt to stem the tide of cruelty, and we can do all of this without failing to learn our needed moral lessons. Therefore, if we can create a less brutal world without making it uninstructive, God could have too. This realization, that he could have and did not, has produced the divine scandal of our age. Mentally deficient human beings are neither needed nor necessary in the scheme of things. God could have eliminated them and evidently chose not to.

Everywhere we turn today our theological question is the same: "Why did you do that?" And in each instance we know enough to be sure that one answer is: It did not have to be that way. Since the same results could be

achieved by other means, what we see in front of us is a
deliberate choice on God's part made in the face of acceptable alternatives. We know in each and every instance
that he must have wanted it just this way and no other, and
this saddles God with full and complete responsibility for
every natural evil and hereditary injustice no matter how
small or how large. In previous centuries men found ways
to excuse God. Now both he and we have grown up. God
has come of age as well as man, and we will have a God
who accepts his full responsibility—as we who read existentialism must too—or else none at all.

In the face of such a charge a new and a "rougher" concept of deity is required to explain God's purposes and
his choices; and, until this is worked out satisfactorily,
many will prefer atheism. Only a strong God, one who
once willed blood sacrifice, is suitable to as much responsibility as we now must make him assume, and the
structure of such a God's mind is not easy to lay bare.
Freud had trouble with man's mind when he discovered
that it works on principles not easily brought into consciousness. What Freud did for man we must in our age
do for God. What can have motivated him to act in the
way that he did in creating our order in the face of an
apparent lack of reasons which justify its deficiencies? We
must make the divine unconscious conscious.

The ironic fact is that in a free system, as man gains
more responsibility for his own actions (which is the
existentialist's message), so does God. This is how it
works: In facing each decision, man has certain alternatives that are greater or lesser in number depending upon
the situation. In calculating the forces involved, man's own
will acts, and in each decision man either accepts or shirks
responsibility for the fact that his will did not choose differ-

ently. For each choice that man makes, God is not responsible. Nevertheless, God did create the framework within which every choice must be made, and he could have willed a world of different situations, different forces, and other odds. He could have given us an alternative set of circumstances as the context for our decisions.

Ours is the individual responsibility for the choice made within the alternatives offered to us. God's is the ultimate responsibility for setting us in that situation in the first place, and this is surely the more powerful and terrible burden. We did not give ourselves our world, but God did, and he must be held accountable for every aspect of it in contrast to its alternatives. Our problem is to find a concept of a God powerful enough to accept this burden and to stand firm in the face of a public scandal.

As if this were not enough, Christianity has also announced another scandal. Any ruling monarch who has a sense of his power and his station respects and rewards those who are strong like himself. People who behave properly and who do as they ought should be the objects of divine affection and favor, and much popular religion amounts to such a moral view. Instead, what Christians claim to have had revealed to them is that God loves *all equally* without distinction of class or race and that he even has a particular compassion for the poor, the inferior, and the despised. This is strange behavior and an odd sentiment for a ruler, and it is a scandal because such a lack of aristocratic discrimination breaks all accepted rules of practice. We love those who love us, and in this world we reward the talented and the successful. Thus, a God who exhibits so complete a lack of aesthetic taste and overturns our sense of justice is a strange and scandalous deity.

His conduct is not a simple matter of total perversion. It is not that God loves only the unworthy and ignores all who are overachievers; that would be too easy. The problem is that Christians say his love is communicated to all without regard, high or low, and that it is available to all irrespective of merit. Elaborately developed protocol is thrown into chaos by this unexpected action. It is not just simply reversed, and who knows who will wind up sitting next to whom at any heavenly dinner party? Such divine dispersion of love violates the known codes of any land; it mixes up princes and paupers and treats alcoholic and reformer alike. To abandon all clear systems of status is a scandalous piece of behavior for a God, since he works against the very world and its hierarchies which he himself created and allowed to develop as they are. Perhaps this is why so many people with justification expect God to be a defender of the *status quo*—i.e., he created it.

The question arises whether the story of this scandal, as it unfolds, is to be judged as a tragedy or a comedy. The harsh judgment of our age is that it must, if evaluated by the score to date, be ruled a tragedy. If we cared less for the unfortunate, this issue would be softened; but, if the poor of the world die by the millions of disease and hunger, we now know how to prevent this but are not able to, while God knows how and could have but did not. This action makes a rather damning drama, and by all tests it ought to be labeled a tragedy. With only a little calculation, every good we know might have been accomplished with less slaughter, suffering, and pain.

Once we thought we might, by our own power, rewrite the script of the world and work at least the last act into a comedy. Today we have the knowledge to do so, but we are uncertain of our ability to carry out our revisions of the text. It is true that the last act has not yet been played, that the final curtain might come down on some surprises and thus turn the play into a comedy, but, judging from the action we have seen thus far, it does not appear that this will happen. In our day God must answer for more than he has ever been held responsible for before, but it is not clear what kind of God is either capable of giving such strong replies or accepting such horrendous burdens upon himself.

Comparing these three sources of divine scandal, the incarnation of God in human form no longer presents so severe a problem. Given some conceptions of God, his appearance in human form may be difficult to conceive, but we have worked at theology long enough so that we have formed concepts of God which make such a change not beyond reason's ability to grasp. The second source of scandal, i.e., that God should not support the very value structures in the world which he created, that the thief might be equal to the priest in God's eyes—in a democratic era it is not as hard to accept this as divine behavior as it was in an age of kings.

Yet, if we do not count it as scandalous that God does not give rewards according to the world's standards, accepting this behavior does depend on the third scandal: that today we refuse to take the world's structure for granted. This being so, it is easy to see that God might not mirror or be identified with any given set of values, since values are no longer thought to reduce to only one scale or order. Nevertheless, this only intensifies the pressure of the third scandal: If nothing about the structure and the order of values among which we live is necessary, why did God create a structure more brutal and more harsh than needed to achieve any moral aim?

For instance, consider the question of God and pain. If the task of theodicy is to justify the ways of God to man, the scandal involved becomes most graphic in the problem of pain. When our means to alleviate physical and mental suffering were few, then we accepted the presence of pain with less protest. Now that we are able to relieve suffering and to calm the tortured mind by drugs, we wonder why God did not do more to lessen this burden in his original design of the world. Perhaps more than any other evil or difficulty, pain is a problem in this respect just because it is so "democratic." That is, it descends on the good and bad alike, on the virtuous as well as on the profligate. Pain is no respecter of persons; it falls like rain on both the just and the unjust. If it were dealt out proportionately, or even if it were given as reward and punishment, we could understand its presence better. As it is, its severity often leads us either to a cruel God or to none at all.

Ironically, good men seem more humane than God where the relief of pain is concerned. In the story of the good Samaritan, Jesus recommends that we evidence our love of God by ministering to the needs of those in distress. Not all men are so kind or so willing to risk themselves for their neighbors, but some are, and they spend their lives relieving pain and suffering. God, at least at present, apparently does less than the best men. It is true that he designed a world in which it is possible for men to devise ways to relieve pain. Yet some very simple solutions were centuries in coming, and their discovery could have been made easier by the original design of the world. Furthermore, whatever good purposes suffering promotes —and I do not deny that there are some—this instruction could easily have been accomplished with a lesser amount of pain. It is the *degree* of pain inflicted on the world which is the hardest decision that God must be made to account for.

What makes the issue even more complex is that we cannot say that God does nothing about pain. If we think he will do something about it in the future, this does not change the present situation or erase the fact that millions have already suffered beyond relief. For the moment let us leave out of account any future change which God might bring about through his own action and consider only in what ways God might be said to have acted to relieve pain both now and in the past.

The first thing to note here is that his action is at least unclear, and it is subject to both debate and misunderstanding. In whatever ways he has acted, not all men see his action as unmistakable, so that the least we can say is that he moves quietly and not openly. No one has seen God stoop to relieve suffering as we have seen some men do, although it is equally true that the first thing we must say is that he created men who are neither wholly impervious to suffering nor so callous that none respond to cries of help.

More men could be more sympathetic than they are by nature, so that we must still hold God responsible for the degree of selfishness incorporated in human nature. By naturally available remedies, some pain can be relieved, so that God did open a few sources of alleviation to us. This does not account for why some remedies are so hidden or took so long to discover, nor does it explain why some means of relief are linked to such dubious side effects, e.g., drugs coupled to addiction. Yet avenues of relief were provided within the world's original plan, even if we still cannot understand either the small amount of these or their obscurity for centuries.

It is in religious doctrine, however, that we encounter the major claim for God's action on behalf of the sufferer. However, such religious assertions are still not easy to assess or simple to prove in their effectiveness. If religious revelation is God's answer to the problem of pain, it is an interesting solution to consider, but it is one that does not come without raising a host of questions of its own. Why, for instance, did he choose to offer himself only to a small group rather than to everyone simultaneously? If we can solve the problem of instantaneous universal communication, God certainly could have too, and he need not have limited his disclosure to a few Jews.

We are left with both the degree and the amount of physical suffering, plus the slowness of our discovery of various remedies, as evidently being the situation in which God knowingly chose to place us. Once his decision was made, we are on our own. However, Christianity has announced the availability of a relief from suffering, at least in some forms, and that source of release needs more examination where God is concerned. To do this, let us set aside the extraordinary case of a physical miracle. This is neither to affirm nor to deny the possibility of miracles but simply to note that this avenue of relief, by very definition, must be used only infrequently. Therefore, miracles do not enter into our consideration of the bulk of pain, since this source of relief must always be minor in comparison to the need. Any relief from suffering which Christianity promises must essentially be different in kind from a series of physical miracles, although nothing prevents these from accompanying the announcement of its message.

Let us for the moment also rule out any promise for future relief, change, or restoration, although admittedly this is to leave out a lot. Much of the optimism of religion does take the form of a reliance on a radical alteration which God will make in the structure of things in the future. However, we cannot check on this now. Instead, God must be trusted, and in that sense his promise does little to moderate the present level of pain. Granted that God placed us in this less than favorable situation, we also want to know what avenues of relief religion can offer in the present.

In order to answer this question, the first thing to note is the existence of a belief in future relief and in the opening up of more favorable circumstances—this in itself helps us to bear pain with greater fortitude, and it also provides a certain degree of present relief. The belief that "the Kingdom" is already within and among us works to change our discouraged attitude which might otherwise succumb in the face of present pain. Of course, if the future promise does not materialize, this would prove to be a false relief, but it is still true that belief in such an ultimate avenue of escape fortifies our ability to withstand pressure now.

We know that the level, degree, and amount of pain, plus the accessibility of remedies, each could have been greater or lesser. If we fix the levels where he did, we surmise that he must have wanted us to work within the present range. Although that decision seems more severe than necessary to accomplish any good lesson that can be learned from pain, what is even harder to understand are some of the troubling complications involved in the available sources of relief. Amazingly enough, each avenue of relief is almost as full of danger as the pain itself. Food, sex, drugs, and alcohol are all good examples of the dilemma. Each relieves a degree of pain and is momentarily satisfying, and yet each one also involves problems of its own when resorted to repeatedly or used in quantity. The side effects often lead to more pain than the original difficulty, and no built-in scale of moderation comes with these remedies. The situation seems intentionally designed to lead us astray easily, since each remedy can be used in moderation only with great difficulty. It would seem that the least we might ask God for is to have provided us with less dangerous sources of relief from pain.

However, it is almost more important to understand that the problem becomes more serious over psychological or spiritual pain rather than physical. Physical pain rarely seems to drive us to excess, whereas the sufferings of the troubled spirit—and the ambitions of the greedy—these situations more naturally trap us into uncontrolled excesses. Is it perhaps here that Christianity can provide more immediate relief without depending on a promise of future restoration? How can any religious doctrine do this, and what insight does this provide into the presence of pain? How can a physical being discover what the needs of his spirit are and how they can be satisfied? *When pain is present, then one becomes aware of needs that might otherwise go unrecognized.* Pain can focus attention on the spirit which all too easily could remain unseen. Unfortunately, however, if these needs are not recognized as spiritual, we can still lose ourselves in trying one form of physical relief after another.

When pain appears, that seems to be the moment when the human spirit can be seen and understood; but it is also a time when it can, unfortunately, be even more easily lost in the rush to find immediate relief. In such a dangerous situation, if Christian doctrine could provide a relief from pain, it would seem that this would also allow the soul to stand out clearly against its physical surroundings. A God who would provide a way out of psychological pain is at least more understandable than one who provides none. This does not at all explain either the *degree* of physical pain that he has inflicted on us or the slenderness and the complexities of the escape routes that are open to us. However, at least it does provide evidence for a God who is not beyond care and concern. Should he himself participate in pain, this might enable us to accept the limits imposed upon us with just a shade less protest. And, if by sharing physical pain, God can be said to overcome it, this would open up new avenues of escape to us, even though we do not possess the sustaining power of a God.

If psychologically we learn that pain can be overcome by enduring it, perhaps religious awareness can make clear the dangers involved in trying to escape. This does not mean either that we should seek pain unnecessarily or fail to relieve it when the remedy is simple. It may mean that some spiritual sources of pain cannot be gratified physically without the danger of addiction to the remedy in every increasing quantity. In the midst of pain we can learn to separate physical from spiritual suffering, and this is a needed lesson if we are to avoid a physical addiction to the remedy. Then there is at least the possibility that a psychological pain can be dealt with nonphysically. Perhaps our greatest problems lie in not recognizing what the cause of the pain is, since mental pains are as real as physical pains and also are less avoidable. Thus, if we do not know how to deal with it, pain can easily destroy us, but it can also make the self stand out more clearly in its extraphysical dimension.

Still, however it is understood, the problem of pain is a graphic illustration of the divine scandal in our time. In

an earlier day when we could not relieve pain except
clumsily, and when the order of the world and its afflic-
tions seemed necessary, then man could simply bear pain
religiously. Now we are shocked to find that God might
have taken routes to avoid so much pain and that he imposed it on men anyway. Remedies with fewer difficulties
involved in their administration might have been devised
and they were not.

Nowhere more than in pain does the question of God's
decision to structure the world in its present form come
under serious question. It is true, as we have pointed out,
that in the midst of this we sometimes confuse spiritual
with physical suffering and then sink deeper into trouble
because we do not understand the source of pain and so
apply the wrong medication. In the midst of pain, we can
come to see a new direction clearly and be converted to
spiritual matters, but we can also become further confused
and drift into deeper despondency over the wrong remedies. The alternatives and the distinctions were not set out
very clearly for all men to see in the first place.

As the modern world opened before us, we hoped at
first to answer our problems once and for all. Where the
existence of pain is concerned, we may learn new remedies,
but its very existence in extreme and complicated forms
stands out as a constant item of unfinished discussion between God and man. In pain we want to know, "God, why
did you do that?" and it is now clear that, in shaping a
reply, either we will discover a God strong enough to bear
the burden of pain and to inflict it on others or else we will
lose a former God and have none at all.

The crucial issue in the possible discovery of a new God
in the midst of pain hinges on his ability to experience pain
and suffering himself. This is something which it was im-

possible for God to do according to most classical accounts, since a traditional doctrine of God thought it impossible to attribute any change to him. The "God of pain" must by nature be capable of feeling, but he must also be able to explain the reasons for his choice of the exact degree and confusion of pain that we face. Even when he offers us a remedy now, we still want to understand why its coming was so long delayed. Here is the heart of the divine scandal; and here also is the center where religion is either made or broken and where Gods are lost or found.

Chapter 3

THE ANSWER TO HUME

Of all the literature that seems to decide against the existence of God, Hume's *Dialogues Concerning Natural Religion*[10] is certainly one of the classics. Like most that is first-rate in philosophy, it is, of course, a mistake to say that its conclusions are totally negative. A philosopher grasps the complexity and the difficulty of a problem so that it becomes clear to both the writer and the reader alike just why this is a difficult problem, why it has persisted, and why its solution is not an easy matter. With varying degrees of assurance, a philosopher may indicate a solution with a measure of certainty. However, the reader must recognize that it is a solution only within the framework which that philosopher has been skillful enough to create; it depends upon the basic assumptions of that view of philosophy for its solving power. Not to recognize this would be blindness on the part of either writer or reader.

Hume chose to write in the classical dialogue form, and this indicates his indirect approach to the question of God's existence. However, it often seems to be forgotten that Hume is only considering one very special form of argument in religion. He discusses not all possible arguments for God but only the one that claims *from natural phenomena alone* to be able to reach certain conclusions about

50

God and his nature. Most religions, certainly Christianity, base their own beliefs very little on this argument alone and very much on other sources, e.g., sacred literature, church tradition, the testimony of disciples, revelatory events, personal conversion, etc. Even when considered philosophically and theologically, the basis of religious argument is seldom as "natural" as the way Hume poses it. Whatever different forms of argument there may be, it is still the case that many discover in Hume's *Dialogues* a central problem involved in every consideration of God. We should not think that all theological arguments take Hume's form or accept his principles (e.g., an implicit reference to "the life of habit" or "impressions and ideas" as tests for validity), but it is true that in the *Dialogues* some of the central factors leading to atheism are made clear.

For example, it seems obvious that a simple and casual observation of the world need not lead you to God, particularly if every other source of information is excluded. Nothing prevents a given individual from believing in the existence of a God—this is Hume's point—but nothing compels all reasonable men to accept such a conclusion either. Some good qualities do appear in nature, but brutality, starvation, disease, and destruction are equally obvious natural phenomena. If we have in mind a very peaceful and quietly pious kind of God, it seems clear that no such deity will become quickly evident merely from reciting a catalog of natural events. Hume, of course, faced a period of sentimental romanticism about the goodness of "Nature," so that equally at issue here is the question of whether "Nature" is all sweet and kind or whether it is a little more mixed and ambiguous in itself. If, like Hume, we recognize the brutality of nature, then in itself "Nature"

leaves the basic question of its possible divine origin unde-
cided, since it offers evidence on both sides of the issue
simultaneously.

If it is true, as is here supposed, that Hume's major point
is that the processes of nature when taken in themselves
are inconclusive about God's intentions, what positive conclusions if any can be drawn from this? Hume's is a skep-
tic's argument, and it often has been interpreted by a majority as being negative in its conclusions. However, first
we might ask what assumptions his conclusions rest upon
and then inquire what lessons might be learned about God
by this indirection.

Hume, and all the participants in the *Dialogues,* do accept "sense impressions" as the chief criterion for evidence. Thus, if you differ from Hume on this philosophical
premise, at least the weight given to his arguments might
vary. If you follow the particular account of sense impressions which Hume offers as his theory of knowledge,
you have an excellent example of how the conclusions you
can reach are restricted by that basis. In fact, it is often
hard to see the real implications of a basic philosophical
premise until you observe how a particular first principle
either opens or closes certain conclusions as a specific
philosophical question is considered. God is a good test
case, because considering him brings one's basic philosophical orientation quickly to the surface.

When God becomes an issue, then men choose up sides,
and not every question has such a sharp catalytic effect.
Since he is not a simple item of immediate experience, God
can only be dealt with (like the basic particles of matter)
on a level of premise and inference. Thus, when God is
under discussion, the first principles of a philosophical
operation must be introduced immediately or else the argu-

ment cannot proceed. The ways in which inferences are to be made, and the function of reason in the process all must be set forth or else further consideration ceases. Not every argument for God proceeds this obviously, nor are first principles always set forth so clearly as they are by Hume, but this same process goes on beneath the surface whenever God is considered. To avoid accepting the unacceptable, the first thing a reader must do—whether consciously or unconsciously—is to discover the premises and the structure of the argument about God. Next, he must realize that, in philosophy, these are almost more the issue than God himself, although questioning God draws the assumptions out into the open.

Yet God ultimately is an issue too, Hume also teaches us, and perhaps he is the most important one in the long run. Not a great deal is said about God very directly in the *Dialogues,* so that the first thing which must be done is to extract from the discussion the view, or views, of God's nature which the argument assumes. If the evidence— even Hume's entirely natural observation—seems to argue against the existence of such a God, you may either surrender that concept or else go to work to form or reform a new concept.

In Hume's *Dialogues* (and in most discussions of God) the concept itself tends to remain fixed and the arguments swirl around this already established point. Hume does suggest some rather wild notions of God, but he leaves these completely undeveloped. For target practice and for basic training, exercise on a fixed point is simplest, but in actual fact in theology the target not only moves, it also changes its form. We can still learn a great deal from Hume's discussion, even if it does move around a fixed concept of God. What this rigidity teaches us is that we should vary the concept of God itself depending on the objections raised; we must discern from the way the argument goes just how the concept itself ought to be reformed in order to be functional.

For instance, Hume argues that the world, if accepted simply on face value, has too many imperfections to lead us naturally to a perfect God. The design of the universe has its faults and its apparent blunders, so that the evidence does not of itself suggest an all-good God. Evil and malfunction are all too obvious features of our experience to be ignored, so that any "argument from design" can lead to a somewhat inept and malevolent architect. Hume takes the sentimentally pious God of romantic religion and finds that the world of nature argues as much against as it does for such a simple God. What Hume never does is to ask whether a different concept of God might do any better in the face of the world's imperfections. The goods of the world simply do not lead us to an all-good God. Evil is too prominent and an improved order of creation is all too possible.

Our choice is always between no God and another concept of God. Although Hume's argument does not force only one answer upon us, if we conclude the issue on the side of a negative judgment, this means we deem that particular concept of God to be unacceptable in that respect and for those reasons. Then, using these same reasons, we can reverse Hume's procedure and ask whether there is a concept of God suitable to the very arguments which led to the rejection of the previous one.

It may be, of course, that no concept of God can be constructed to fit the requirements of the problems which led to the rejection of a previous concept, but we will never know unless we try. Once the attempted construction of a new concept has been made, we can see what premises and assumptions are needed to support this new view. At the outset, we learn what first principles and assumptions lead Hume's reader to reject God as incompatible with imperfection in nature, and then we can move on from there to question both our philosophical assumptions and our original notion about God.

Our "answer to Hume" takes the form of bringing clearly to light the framework of philosophy upon which his arguments rest for their support. Then, in place of the concept of God implicit in the original discussion, we substitute a series of modified concepts to see whether another, more acceptable God can be found to replace the one rejected. In this trial and substitution method, the principles and rules of procedure for philosophy shift and reform too, so that at the same time we become sensitive to, and must be prepared to decide between, ways of procedure in philosophical analysis and construction. When we sense the power of the conclusions which become possible on the basis of any selected philosophical mode, there is an impulsive tendency to take the principles formed and simply extend them into a series of conclusions. Doing that will yield some enlightenment, but the source of real insight lies in exploring the foundations of the framework and in learning how conclusions shift as principles of procedure in philosophy are themselves altered. Each major philosopher seems to know this and to be aware that he must give an account of how he forged his own first principles in the course of following precisely this same procedure. Rejecting a conclusion which he seems driven to on one basis, a Hume or a Kant refuses simply to proceed; he turns back-

ward and experiments in basic reformulation until he can
find a workable set of principles and assumptions which
allow different conclusions to be reached.

Unfortunately, most who follow these explorers merely
expand the newer territory which the original philosopher
has opened up and add no new basic insights. However, if
we listen carefully, Hume tells us his answer—which is the
same as our answer to Hume—"State carefully the form
of procedure which you allow and then construct the kind
of concept of God you intend to consider." If you do not
like the conclusion, change your assumptions—blame
neither Hume nor God for some particular conception of
either philosophy or deity.

Now, when it comes to our proposed "divine interrogation" about evil, what have we learned from this "answer
to Hume"? If we want God to tell us why he elected to
create all things as he did, we know that the answer will
vary according to the concept of God which is employed.
Furthermore, we know that no answer can be derived from
the simple observation of natural phenomena. This brings
us to the concept of philosophy involved. On the basis of,
for instance, a sense-data empiricism it is not possible
to go beyond that base. Some philosophical views will not
allow theological answers to be developed and others admit
only answers of a certain type.

In his *Dialogues,* Hume is very interested in the problem
of evil and theodicy, but our "answer to Hume" is to reject an empirical context as incapable of allowing an adequate response to be developed. Given Hume's ground,
God is at a disadvantage in defending himself. When one
observes this, one must next turn to see what kind of view
of God one is operating with and what it will allow. Theodicy begins with an "answer to Hume," that is, with an

examination of the philosophy presupposed and with an increased awareness of how the view of God employed affects the answer that God will give when he is interrogated. Perhaps no philosopher more than Hume wants his readers to discover what they can and cannot conclude on the basis of the assumptions which they have accepted.

In considering Hume's *Dialogues,* we can easily see that he did not pay much attention to various alternatives concerning the nature of God. He was not a theologian and so did not enter into this kind of new construction. He does pay much more direct attention to the issue of philosophical method, and with a little care it is easy to see how his theory of "impressions and ideas" is crucial to the whole consideration. This is as it should be with a philosopher, but Hume's basis does not allow us to accept any other source, such as metaphysics or Scripture, in order to develop a theory about God. Thus, it is not possible to alter the view of God which emerges in order to see if a better answer to the questions can be achieved by using a different notion of deity. Where theodicy is concerned, the issue is often between having no God or being forced to shift our concept of God. Since Hume does not do the latter, the philosophical basis of the *Dialogues* inclines the reader toward a rejection of God due to the problem of theodicy.

In order to answer Hume we have to ask: Can a view of God's nature be developed which might satisfy Hume's complaints? We have already noted that this cannot be done on his own philosophical basis, so we know that the metaphysical principles assumed are the first thing to be examined when we run into theological problems. For example, Hume's attitude on miracles indicates another roadblock, since he states that, in any matter of dispute, one should always side with the majority of common experience. It is possible that a special and unique form of experience might be more true, but, in order to maintain this, we must first construct a standard against which to test experience different from the one which Hume employs. Whenever any answer in theodicy is unsatisfactory, we need to back off and to consider the elements which went together to yield that answer, in order to go on to find a way to restructure the question.

The imperfections in the world do not in themselves lead to a very impressive God; Hume is right. How, then, can we construct a more adequate description of God and still take account of those faults in the world which seem to lead men away from God more often than to him? If the faults that Hume describes are not explained, there is no answer to him. This can be accomplished both by having a God who is able to account for imperfection and by pointing out the variety of philosophical alternatives which are open to the theologian. Hume's God never replies to the questions which the *Dialogues* ask. Perhaps now it is time for philosophers to find a new way to speak for God when he is challenged.

Leibniz[11] makes one of the famous attempts to explain God's actions, and perhaps a brief comparison with Hume might be instructive at this point. In order to interpret Leibniz' famous doctrine that we occupy "the best of all possible worlds," we must understand the philosophical context in which that conclusion is set. Our aim here is not to consider either that doctrine or its context in detail but only to point out one feature of it as illustrative of our conclusion concerning Hume. Leibniz' rationalism is such as to allow only one alternative, and, in considering God's action in creation, perhaps the single most important question is whether God has at least several rational alternatives.

Thomas Aquinas and Leibniz, vs. Spinoza and Plotinus, recognize that the possible modes of being are vastly wider than the modes which were in fact actualized by creation. What is in itself possible is much more than can simply be accounted for as potential within our existing structure. In creating one form, God dooms other forms to perpetual nonexistence, but the more important point is: Does God's reason lead him to one and only one selection? Whatever criteria (e.g., goodness) may guide his reason, still, as a reasonable being, are more choices than one open to him, or do reason and goodness guide him to only one result?

Leibniz seems to answer that reason must be sufficient unto itself and is essentially the single principle responsible for selecting the modes of being to be actualized. The kind of view of philosophy that Leibniz employs leads him to this theological conclusion. It may be that reason does the selecting and considering of alternatives and that it works in accordance with recognized standards (e.g., compatibility, beauty, variety, self-sustenance). Still, although this limits considerably what can be created as compared with what is merely possible, within that range several alternatives (or at least more than one) could still remain. On the basis of rationality alone, each is reasonable; and on the basis of goodness, each has certain advantages. Within this range reason must work, but it is not of itself driven to a single conclusion as alone good or reasonable. This is a possible view, but it is not Leibniz'. It merely illustrates how the philosophical context tends to shape—or at least to restrict—the theological answers where theodicy is concerned.

Our "answer to Hume" was twofold: to question the

sense empiricism or "the life of habit" which he often assumes as a standard of reference for the discussion, and to ask whether his view of God is one which is adequate to deal with the objections that he raises. Similarly for Leibniz, it is his rationalistic framework which is the most important factor in his theodicy. Can an end be achieved—consistent with both reason and goodness—in more than one way? To accept certain solutions would be unreasonable, e.g., to create a world containing factors which are not compossible so that the creation as a whole is abortive —although we do find areas of such fundamental conflicts within an order which itself is not basically subject to that fault. Reason sifts standards and values and excludes some, although God in his own thought stands above the law of noncontradiction, for instance, and applies it to his thought concerning creation. Our thought is able to move in ways other than that embodied in creation (e.g., three-valued logics); but, fortunately, our reason is not quite as free in its form as is God's.

If an end cannot be achieved rationally in more than one way, and if goodness is not irreducibly plural—which seems to be Leibniz' view—the way in which we understand God's relation to the world will be quite different where theodicy is concerned. Given Leibniz' rationalism, we are driven to a "best of all possible worlds" as the only alternative to an irrational God. Yet, if our world does not quite seem to fit that philosophical conclusion, our "answer to Leibniz" must take the form of questioning his metaphysics. This, of course, is a very good metaphysical thing to do.

In thinking about God, and in attempting to answer the problem of theodicy, we see that first principles are most important, especially given the limitations of the empirical content available as applicable to this question. If in creation more than one alternative is open to God rationally, if an end can be achieved in more ways than one, and if value norms guide considerations but do not always determine them—then the questions of theodicy take on a new light. Hume gives us his own answer where theodicy is concerned. We must reply to him by asking: What other philosophical bases might allow God to explain his actions to us and in what ways?

However, before we can begin to answer that question (Chapter 6), let us face one other encounter with God over the problem of evil, i.e., Jung's consideration of Job. After that we will try to say something about the methodology which is being employed (Chapter 5) in this attempt to find a God who can account for evil. It is not so much that we adopt a certain methodology at the outset as that, embroiled in the question of evil, we are forced to test various means for extricating ourselves from that problem. The method develops as we begin to explore what solutions are open to us, given evil as we find it and a God who can begin to emerge from its midst.

Chapter 5 will outline a little of the kind of metaphysics which emerges in this essay. Of course, like God, it is not a question of starting with a view full-blown. Instead, the problem of interrogating God arises, and then answers like Hume's are suggested. At that point it begins to become clear what kind of assumptions lead to what kind of answers; and, if a new solution is glimpsed and a new God is disclosed, all this comes at the same time that a new view of philosophy is formed which correlates with it. The two processes go together. Basic metaphysics is developed as the adopted method of approach to God becomes clarified. However, let us first see what other assumptions come to the surface if we consider another defense which has often been given for God.

Chapter 4

JOB'S ANSWER TO JUNG

C. G. Jung undoubtedly is one of the more creative and suggestive writers of our century. In contrast to Freud, he lends a sympathetic ear and gives a sensitive reception to religious matters. Freud is a rationalist of the Spinozist school, whereas Jung is more to be understood in the Neoplatonic tradition. It is interesting to see how different the philosophical contexts are for the two major psychiatric theories of our time. However, where theodicy is concerned, Jung's *Answer to Job*[12] offers a fascinating new slant.

Essentially, Jung is shocked by the Biblical account of God's behavior in his relation to Job, and he sees the incarnation as God's attempt to atone for his guilt in treating Job so badly. Usually the incarnation has been interpreted as God's voluntary effort to atone for man's sins, and this is a thing which man is not able to do, at least according to Anselm's *Cur Deus Homo*.[13] In Jung's account, on the other hand, God is overcome by a sense of guilt which results from his unjust treatment of Job. He has allowed Satan to punish Job when Job has, apparently, done nothing but live a righteous life. Thus, God becomes man and suffers in order to work out his (God's) guilt. That is Jung's account, and, compared with that, Anselm's theory of the incarnation is quite different indeed. Classically it is said that none but man needs to repay a debt and none but God is able to repay what he does not owe.

Jung's God is clearly of a quite different type from Anselm's; a divine darkness is unveiled in Jung's interpretation of Job. However, our concern here is to see whether Job has any reply to give to Jung. Is there an answer to be made for God which Jung has overlooked in his solicitude for Job's suffering? Jung's God is depicted as still "unconscious" in his encounter with Job, and thus he has not yet become moral. That will happen later on, and it will account for the difference between Job and Jesus. Jung's God matures from an early primitiveness. Job is guiltless, according to Jung, and, thus, he achieves a knowledge superior to God's unawareness.

However, it is interesting to note that Jung's attitude toward God's action is quite different from Job's own response. Jung is incensed over God's unfair treatment when God makes a bargain with Satan, and he interprets the incarnation as a growth in consciousness and as a change in God toward becoming a moral being. In the Biblical account, however, Job is represented as uncomplaining and as accepting God's strange treatment without reproach. It is only Job's "friends and comforters" who suggest that he rebel against the suffering which God has allowed to be visited upon him. This temptation Job rejects, and he remains faithful to God through all the trials. Jung's attitude is much more modern than either Job's or Anselm's. In the original story, Job is portrayed as a faithful and righteous man, and yet, in a bargain with Satan, God allows everything to be stripped away from Job in order to test his faithfulness against Satan's challenge to God. Today, it is true, men do seem less inclined to accept their lot without complaint. They will not allow God to treat them as he wills without interrogating God as to the reasons for what he does.

Of course, this is not true of everyone today, and neither were all in Job's age as unrebellious as he (his friends illustrate that this is so). Some people can accept suffering in silence in our post-Biblical time without rejecting God. This points up one central factor which Jung seems to leave out of his account. (Although it is true that the context within which we consider theodicy has changed in the time from Job to Jung.) What Jung cannot seem to allow for is the attitude of religious faith. However, given our attitude toward the world, we are less likely than Job to understand such faith and therefore are more inclined to join with Jung in protesting God's unfair action.

Job at certain times did ask God questions concerning his treatment. Yet the answers that are given for God do not justify his actions, but instead turn the tables and deny Job's right even to question God. Job's attitude on the whole is portrayed as one of acceptance, and this is something which we can no longer do very easily. We are more likely to demonstrate and to protest rather than to accept silently. We are prone to side with Jung in his view of the meaning of incarnation, i.e., that God, overcome by guilt in his treatment of man, himself suffers in order to atone and to grow in moral consciousness.

The writer of the Book of Job probably never questioned the kind of world in which he had been set. Now we are aware that it is possible to alter the structure and to achieve more favorable conditions, and we wonder why God refused to do at least what man seems able to do for others. We want to have explained to us a world that is less favor-

able than necessary. When we fight within a system that
is more negative than it need be, we question whether it
must be that way. Not that our world as given is without
its advantages; it could be much worse than it is, i.e., so
destructive as either to make life impossible or any form
of beauty unachievable. We are actually even more aware
of the intricacies and the potentials which are present
within our structure as it is given to us. *Yet perhaps it is
just because we see how much can be done to create more
favorable conditions for man that we are also more aware
that we were not given the most optimum circumstances
for life which were possible.* God seems to have drawn the
line at least a little lower than necessary, and we wonder
why.

Where theodicy is concerned, we must allow Job to
speak. In order to understand religious faith, Kierkegaard
takes Abraham as his example.[14] From both Abraham and
Kierkegaard it is always possible to learn religious pro-
fundity, but Job actually seems more appropriate to our
day, and perhaps he can teach us a needed lesson. Kierkegaard's example centers the meaning of faith around "ab-
surdity." Abraham is commanded by God to act in such
a way that he apparently destroys what God has himself
given to him, that is, his son Isaac. To follow God's command means to act against all normal ethical standards.
This "suspends the ethical" and places the obedient believer outside of all possible justification. Thus, the believer
is absolutely isolated in faith. His behavior makes it impossible for him to explain himself to anyone else, since
he acts outside of all norms. He stands alone, unsure that
he actually is a man of faith but committed to act, i.e., to
take the leap of faith (in this case to sacrifice Isaac on

lem as that of a God who designs a world, one which is not without its good features, but a world more violent and less just than he might have selected. In the face of this, Jung indicts God for inflicting unjustified suffering. What can Job possibly answer to Jung?

Job can teach Jung the meaning of religious faith, and this is a factor which Jung omits. Yet, that is only the beginning of the matter and not the end of it in our time. Kierkegaard accuses us all of not being willing to stop with faith and of always wanting to go farther, but the issue is not quite that simple. Man may in the end lack a definitive answer, that is, one which lacks the necessity needed to settle the matter conclusively, but religious faith has meaning only when we understand our situation and know how far we can and cannot go toward a full explanation. Only as we arrive at some clarity about the nature of God and give some account of why he acts toward man as he does—only then is it really possible to see what is required of and left to religious faith. We can hardly be faithful until we understand what specific attitude "faith" involves. For us, this may mean to understand either God's actions toward Job or the reason why God elects a world no more suited to justice than it is. Jung thinks that God feels guilty over the undeserved punishment of Job which was inflicted in God's more primitive moral state, but that objection assumes a God who deals out rewards perfectly according to merit and on the basis of immediate rewards for superior performance. If it is set in a broader context, perhaps God's action is not so "immoral" after all.

"Hang on!" seems to be Job's message, but that is not enough in itself. We need to understand what kind of God can deal with men in a harsh way without either betraying them (as Jung thought) or being less than divine. We seem faced with a God who deals with us silently, if brutally, at times. Of course, no one needs to believe in such a God. Religious faith means to see God in this way and not to reject him but to accept him. This being the case, we can perfectly well understand why many, perhaps even a majority, will prefer to deny God rather than accept this kind of God. Of course, this is not all of the story. The religious man continues to believe in God just because he does not see the present situation as final. He places his trust in a sign and a promise given by God of a future which will be different. However, a sign and a promise cannot be proven in advance. Even if partially present, they can only be believed in. If the future is discounted, as it is by Jung, the present situation may be such as to indict God on moral grounds.

Such faith in future justice in the face of present inequalities and brutalities—this is precisely what many men cannot accept. They prefer to work without God and to do what they can do by themselves to change an originally unfair situation. By its nature no promise, not even God's, can be guaranteed beyond all doubt, and, therefore, this very condition will cause as many or more to doubt as it will to believe. Religious faith means to remain steady in spite of the icy blast, although in order to do this many— not all—need to understand why the situation is structured in this way. "Faith seeking understanding" is too simple a formula to apply here, for in order to believe one must first fathom at least what is demanded of him. For us this may mean to go beyond Job and to see if we can come to visualize the divine nature in such a way that his action in inflicting unearned suffering becomes, if not necessary, then at least understandable.

It is likely that Job understood quite clearly the nature

eventually restored to health and wealth and family. Yet, even without this happy ending, Job's outcome is not quite strong enough to solve our present argument with God. Job is successful and prominent, and he is also a man already gifted with religious understanding. Suffering applied to him is not pleasant, but at least it can serve to bring out the real solidity of his religious faith. Without a lowering into the depths, religious faith in favorable circumstances remains insecure and vague. The testing of a strong and noble man is edifying, and we can understand a kingly God who operates in that way. But the world has few Jobs and many more inherently weak peasants.

Consider not Job, but his uneducated subnormal kitchen servant (a Faulkner-type hero). Struck down by a cart in the street, maimed and helpless in the face of adversity —his talents and strengths are too few and too weak to bear the forces placed upon him, and he breaks. This does not describe a testing of religious faith, because the circumstances never even gave this poor creature a chance to form one. We learn of this kind of evil each day, and it bothers us because it is so useless.

Of course, it is true that religious faith is a democratic affair, no more to be found among the rich and the gifted than among the poor and the underprivileged. It may appear in any circumstances, and yet the destructive forces in the world are stronger than are necessary in order to produce religious edification. They are unfair in the sense that they are sometimes too strong to give the person subjected to them even a fighting chance. For Job to suffer may serve some purpose, but to crush his ignorant kitchen boy or to sweep a helpless child downstream—in this case God seems to have applied a pressure greater than necessary. God has given free reign to forces that are capable of destroying faith and confidence rather than building and testing them. *It is this situation which requires the more difficult explanation.*

Job can reply to Jung and teach him the meaning of both obedience and the necessity for testing as part of religious faith, but that is only a partial answer. We must go "beyond Job" in our day if we are to find a ground for faith. Since we do not accept what comes to us as being necessary, we want God to tell us why he allowed most circumstances to be even less favorable than those under which Job questioned him. Job had the advantages of a good religious background; he had enjoyed prosperity and he never lost his ability to speak to God. What about those who never have known prominence or prosperity or whose burdens strike them dumb before they can locate a God to talk to? Job can answer Jung, but who will speak to the questions that still remain after Job has spoken for those who at least once were favored by God? In our day we more often begin by not knowing how to address God.

It is perhaps not true that we live in an age which is any more aware of evil than any other time in man's history. It is just that we follow after an age in which many thought we might overcome evil largely on our own and then see a new era dawn through science and man's creativity. That dream no longer seems true, and we must again learn to live with evil, not so much that it has increased but that it has not disappeared in the face of man's increase in power. Freud, against Jung, is much more likely to think of evil as something that can be overcome by rational and scientific effort. To follow Jung here is not to deny that this is possible in individual cases, but it is to see evil as

Chapter 5

POSSIBLE WORLDS, POSSIBLE GODS, POSSIBLE DEVILS

Empirically-minded philosophers are right; we always do begin with a world that is concretely in front of us. The only problem is that centuries of discussion have not been able to establish whether or not what is presented to us in immediate experience is understandable simply on its own. Philosophers have differed precisely over this point: What else must be added in order to render the world and our experience understandable? No matter how simple they are, none of the suggestions given by philosophers has proved to be automatically acceptable. The appeal to "experience" seems to raise as many questions as it answers.

We are faced with a clear set of facts but also with a number of frameworks within which to interpret them. Not that we need to be the helpless victim of a multiplicity of theoretical frameworks, but we do seem unable to reduce all the types of theory down to one, even if we can narrow the range of acceptable approaches. To accomplish this rational delimiting is philosophy's business. In going about this activity, one cannot assume that methodologies are any more final than are speculative theories. Some modern philosophers thought that a single method could be established, even if metaphysical first principles could not be agreed upon, but trying to settle upon one philosophical method has proved to be no less controversial than metaphysics.

The "phenomenological method" claims to use only what is "given" as its material. Nevertheless, its procedure for analyzing this given material itself raises the primary question, and we have learned that the philosophical terms which we employ are no more neutral or obvious than the method. The physical sciences are not ultimately helpful to us here, since a single theory has not emerged there. If the attempt to achieve such finality and unity has on the whole been given up, we cannot expect help from outside theology. And if no one theoretical context is given to us which we must use, we have no choice but to construct our own and to defend it against a variety of alternatives.

The theory offered below of how the world is to be understood is perhaps at the opposite pole from a strict empiricism; but, in theoretical understanding, our distance from brute fact is always a matter of degree and not one of an absolute departure from all "evidence." Since empirical facts are not self-interpretive, the methodology we use is never neutral, and all theoretical structure is not capable of reduction to one framework. Nevertheless, at least it remains possible that a theory, even one which is detached from simple empiricism, might in fact be the most illuminating and could even provide us with a preferable way of understanding.

We have, according to the account adopted here, one world to start with, but our understanding of it comes from a balance of three variables. The first of these variables is the given world itself, that is, we begin by refusing to take it as simply given. This is a kind of reverse of the phenomenological method. In spite of its obviousness, we

possibility as such. In forming a concept of this single decisive force that moves upon the possibles, more than one
concept is available. This is particularly so since we do
not begin in as favorable a situation here as with the possible worlds where we have only one actual one before us.
True, of all the possible Gods, ours must be such as to
be able actually to have selected the world we know in
preference to all the others. We have that much as a concrete form of reference, but, although the number is reduced and is now manageable, we are still faced with various possible Gods.

As if it were not enough to have to face a variety of
possible concepts of God at the same time that our world
fades out toward becoming merely one among a possibly
infinite series, we must add a third concept for our understanding, i.e., the devil. This must be done because the
world is not made up of all positive and good forces. As
Plato noted in the latter part of *The Republic,* forces of
deterioration and destruction are at work in our world too;
evil must be accounted for as well as good if we wish to
understand the order (and the disorder) in which we are
assigned to live. Like God, the devil may be differently
conceived, and so the third variable concerns possible
devils. It is likely that the centers of possible destruction
are also one, just as there is in fact one God. However,
the sources of destruction and negation are more than one,
and so the devil may be variously conceived just as the
actual variety present in the world allows for God to be
conceived of in many ways.

Possible worlds, possible Gods, possible devils—these
three factors are what we must learn to hold in balance
before any profound understanding of experience can come
into being for us. Since the factors are three and not one,

we know from a reading of Plato's *Parmenides*[17] that any theoretical explanation we form cannot be singular either. More than one theoretical framework will always be possible, and theories will tend toward infinity if not refined by the philosopher and held to some definite number of viable theories. Man himself participates in all three factors; he is a combination of them and not a fourth factor. Still, man has the special function of working with the three basic factors and of balancing them to provide an explanation of how our world came to be with precisely the kind of combination of factors which it represents.

This distinction between the three factors that are necessary in order for understanding to be possible is in some sense artificial. That is, after the distinguishing process, what must finally be grasped is the precise mode of combination of these factors. In speaking of possible Gods, we point to the power of the actualizing force and the attributes that it needs in order to accomplish this selection process. In possible worlds, we indicate the material nature of God upon which he works, and with possible devils we explain that this is not a simple or a smooth process, that the divine nature contains and must contend with internal negative and destructive forces as well as positive. In order to understand the empirical world, we must bring these three factors into some exact relationship, and that ultimately means to be able to conceive of God, since his nature contains all three in some balance.

Partly because of this "third force," God's nature can never be reduced to, or centered completely around, one basic attribute but must always be grasped at least in terms of three. This in itself tells us why we can never reach one final theory of God; some ultimate multiplicity is constitutive of his nature too. Not that we cannot form

combination of several of the fundamental forces which
they have described. Nevertheless, the fact that we have
more views of God than one also leads us on to a multiplicity of possible worlds.

We select a world to match a God and a God to match
all the worlds that we come to see as possible. However,
this concentrates all the positive forces in the concept of
God, whereas it is just as much true that, for every view of
God, there is also a corresponding devil which must be accepted, i.e., if we are to hope to account for the destructive
and negative forces. Spinoza does not give such forces real
status; instead, he views all chaos as only the result of
intellectual confusion. Still, his view of God dictates the
way in which Spinoza will account for the world's violence.
For every idea of God there is a corresponding idea of the
devil; and, if one begins with the negative forces, then from
every concept of the devil an idea of God can also be
shaped accordingly.[19]

The negative forces in our world could be different,
both in kind and in power. From this fact we learn that
other devils are possible too in addition to the one operative
in our world. We must also account for why the destructive forces are not different than they are, why we have the
devil which we have to contend with and not some other
possible one whether greater or lesser in its power. Since
the forces of evil could be other than they are in kind, our
world is just as well explained by its possible devil, in comparison to the others, as it is by its possible God. The
world and God can just as easily be approached from the
negative side as from the positive.

In order to obtain from God an answer to our question,
"Why did you do that?" we find ourselves forced to deal
with an infinity of possible worlds, a variety of Gods, and

a series of devils. Out of this combination alone an answer can come. To accomplish this we must establish a criterion that allows us to select one view of God together with a view of the destructive forces operating, and this must be one that will account for our world's position among all those which are possible. This combination, as we have said, is our triune God, of which the God who has the decisive powers of selection is one part.

Ours is a much more difficult task than if we had only one possible world, one God, and one devil. Explaining this lack of basic simplicity seems to be the only route to an adequate understanding of why God did what he did in creation. Our answers will never be reduced to a single one which is not subject to change, and the multiplicity present in our theories will always prevent necessity from characterizing the resulting account, but we have no other alternative. Faced as we are by possible worlds, possible Gods, and possible devils, we must make a selection before we can begin our divine interrogation. The selection we make—whether we are talking to it, him, or them— will determine the answers given to our questions. What kind of God can possibly answer our questions?

In trying to decide this, we may very well have to come to understand evil first before we can locate God. In some earlier times, men have denied that anything exists which deserves the strong title of "evil," but from many quarters a new appreciation of the continual presence of evil has emerged. Paul Ricoeur thinks that we can come to understand evil by considering the myths which have portrayed it.[20] We need to grasp how evil functions as a symbol, especially since we cannot understand man's relation to the sacred without it (p. 6). We need to "reenact" the experience made explicit by the myth. Consciousness of

Why is it that, to so many, existence itself does not seem good? Augustine seems wrong in his insistence on the natural goodness of existence.

What kind of God can account for this extreme situation and, when we find him, what does he have to say in his own defense? In the first place, a strong God will not be easy to find; and, when and if we do, he is not likely to have much to say to defend himself. The strong do not need to talk. God has not seen fit to defend himself publicly by offering reasons for creating the world as he did, and no simple good purpose can be read off the surface of the kind of existence millions of unfortunate men know.

We are clearly dealing with a hidden God—i.e., one who, if he acts, does so indirectly and leaves his motives and his reasons to be inferred; he is one who does not speak openly to defend his actions. Even when Christians preserve their testimonies and remind us of his claimed appearance and revelation, this is still not enough to remove all doubt. Our centuries of dispute testify that his appearance was not clearly self-evident, and it is still subject to more than one interpretation. However he may have acted and revealed himself, he left behind him a trail of unanswered questions.

We may, it is true, do some interpreting for God as Paul did, and that helps. Still, we are dealing with a God of "willful rationalism," i.e., one who works within reason's bounds but whose will is strong enough to select a more dangerous and difficult and destructive road than any reason alone requires. The rational structure of our order, or at least the part that we can decode, understand, and master, testifies that he was not irrational in creation. Yet on rational grounds there is no reason why the limits of possibility could not have been set elsewhere so that destruction would be minimized.

God willed not an impossible world but one more prejudiced against man than necessary. The food supply could have been a little more evenly distributed, or at least it might have been increased naturally so as to preclude starvation. The ravages of disease might have been lessened just a bit, and population could have been more evenly distributed and more easily controlled. In the world that God elected, some can hold their footing, but others cannot. If God liked only the strong, the brave, and the skillful, his actions would not be so hard to understand. On the other hand, if God, as the Christians claim, cares for each of us alike, the world he designed does not show this generosity clearly. Democracy must be won and maintained against odds; it is not a natural tendency. Rather, our world seems to be a stadium in which to watch the strong and the talented battle for power and success while others less well endowed are caught in between. God's creation does not fit his announced Christian intent, and we must account for this discrepancy, if it is not to be taken as a miscalculation on God's part. This discrepancy can be explained only if we are dealing with a God of will and of ulterior purposes, for his will holds to a line lower than goodness itself can account for. If his intentions are as announced by Christians, he has purposes that are not clearly evident from the design which he gave to the world. He seems to be capable of holding back his ulterior intent and of not displaying it fully on the surface of his creation.

Unfortunately, an ulterior purpose is the hardest kind of all to deal with, and a will that goes farther than necessary is impossible to account for beyond a certain point. A God like this might "explain" our world, but, ironically, this can never be an entirely satisfactory explanation. We want an explanation that tells us why our world had to be just like this and could not have been different, if God's nature and intent are considered. Such finality alone would stop our reason's motion, quiet it permanently, and let it rest contented. Philosophers and theologians have tried for centuries to provide answers that have this quality, but certainty and definiteness are properties that exist within some given intellectual explanation; they are not features of our world itself. They do not seem to characterize man's relationship to the explanations offered, in spite of the fact that, within the argument itself, such certainty may seem to be present for a time.

Some of the responsibility for this can be laid to man's ignorance and to his unwillingness to accept the truth. Still, it is the case that not all honest and intelligent minds accept one answer which is internally certain and necessary. In creating, God himself used a plan more flexible than some which men have proposed in their theories, but the problem is that such explanations cannot hope to possess the property of certitude. In being flexible in his choice of criteria for creation, God ruled out absolute necessity in the world and banished it to the world of thought.

We can "explain" a will that moves beyond necessity and creates less than optimum circumstances, but nothing explains why it stopped at precisely one point rather than another just beyond or just short of its actual resting point. This does not mean that God's will knew no bounds, but rather that the criteria employed only set a range of alternatives. They are not able to specify one point or to yield one and only one way of accomplishing any selected goal.

An ulterior purpose means that the plan we presently

observe in operation need not be necessary. All that is required is that the stated intent not be incapable of being accomplished through the particular order selected. God is powerful enough to accomplish his purpose in any one of a variety of ways, but this means that a simple inspection of the natural order before us will not in itself tell us what that purpose is or was. Based upon the evidence to date, an ulterior purpose is not clear, and it cannot become so until such time as the proposed change is produced.

If we cannot wait for God's ulterior purpose to be accomplished in order to decide what it is, what can be said in the meantime in his defense? His actions, being more extreme than necessary, strain credulity and demand defense even if they cannot yet be fully justified. These not-perfect means which God selected have created a scandal of his own making, and postmodern men have become more painfully aware of this than were their predecessors who took the world's form either for granted or as necessary. If we as men can design more equitable means to achieve God's goal, why was he content with a not-perfect instrument?

God has freely taken upon himself a more dangerous path than necessary, but this choice demands a defense. Until he acts openly or speaks without the possibility of being misunderstood, it will be up to men to defend God, if he is to have a fair trial at all. Theologians and metaphysicians have been appointed as God's public defenders against the popular accusation of "unnecessary roughness" —a tactic which men who are fair try to stop immediately by penalizing the offender. At least sometimes, God's actions require more explanation than man's.

What is the first thing God is likely to say—or to have said for him—in his defense? What he should do is to begin by refusing to allow himself to be judged at this point in time. However, an appeal to a future restoration of damages is the most difficult of all arguments to assess. Yet God ought to be at least strong enough to withstand any immediate negative judgment and at the same time powerful enough to make good on a promise at some as yet undetermined future point in time. Men are not always strong enough to do this. We sometimes are not able to sustain our good purposes even against present adverse criticism, and often we are helpless to accomplish a future promise when the time comes to settle accounts.

These faults evidently must not be God's, that is, if we are to allow him to appeal to the future and to request a stay of judgment. In our planning, we often are the victims of time, and as a result we are forced to act either too soon or too late. If we are to accept his appeal to some ulterior purpose not yet accomplished, God must have perfect control of time in ways that man can never have. We can't be sure about all this, but at least we can see how he must differ from us if he is to succeed in those situations in which we often fail.

To describe a God like this in reply to the question, "What kind of God?" is in one sense an answer and in another sense it is no solution at all. It is an answer in the sense that such a God fits the kind of world we know, since it is one which is littered with destruction and unnecessary waste no matter what good it may be capable of in its optimum state. Some views of God can account for what is best in the world, but not for the worst, or at least not for why evil and destruction are allowed to reach the limits which they do. The God we uncover in answer to our question can "explain" evil, although it is true that this explanation does not remove every question.

There is another sense in which a God whose will is capable of going farther than either reason or his own goals demand will not provide an answer. Where does God's will first draw a line and hold to it? We see that God's will stopped and by its firmness one limit was set. However, immediately after that point we can find no absolute reason why his will could not have gone a step farther and cut destruction's power one degree short of the limit that was in fact set. Of course, if he had gone very much farther he would have rendered impossible the accomplishment of all rational direction and purpose. On the other hand, if he had controlled destruction much more, he would have created a world designed to satisfy romantic souls, but it would also be one less representative of the vast and violent forces moving within the divine life. We can locate and rule out the unacceptable extremes more easily than we can find the actual midpoint where his will cut through all the possibles decisively. The best we can do is to locate the general area in which God's decision was made.

To set the limits for a decision on either side but to have fixed it at a more extreme point than any needed limit itself dictates—all this we can see and accept, but it never satisfies reason fully or provides an answer capable of becoming definitive. Under such a situation we can have *an* answer but not *the* answer, since neither God's reason alone nor the standard to which he appeals was capable of fixing one and only one mold for creation in the first place. The task of creation involves more facets than one, and thus it is at odds with the unity which reason either attempts to impose or ultimately demands for its full satisfaction. Reason can be satisfied but never to its desired limit. The probable answers that we can work out reach neither to infinity nor do they reduce to one. In this in-between land, God lives; and now men must try to adjust their rational demands to meet that fluid situation.

Nietzsche is famous for having urged that some very few strong individuals should live "Beyond Good and Evil." He felt that part of the reason for man's plight was that he had been domesticated and weakened by the sweetness of religion and had lost his energy and his will to live apart from the herd.[22] Today we seem on the verge of achieving Nietzsche's goal. Few believe in fixed moral standards, and many assert their ability to set their own codes of conduct in spite of prevailing mores. We have a generation of people willing to attempt to live beyond good and evil and to hold their own individual positions there. Now as it develops, in trying to ask what kind of God created conditions as they are, we are struck by the fact that he can best be found beyond good and evil.

If we accept the standards for judging success as we find them given in human society, God is a failure in his ability to create a world in which more than a few can succeed. Furthermore, he is so far beyond good and evil that he would not let himself be totally bound by the usual meanings of "good" in creating the best possible world he could. He held himself aloof from that demand, and so it would seem that he will only be understood when we are able to locate him beyond the restrictions of our immediate notions of what good behavior is like. Nietzsche wanted us to release man from moral bondage. But man is not strong enough to survive there alone. It is only God who is beyond good and evil as he decides on the goals of creation.

Chapter 7

"BECAUSE I WANTED TO!"

To the question, "Why did you do that?" the title of this chapter is ultimately the form that God's reply must take, although the situation is more complex than any simple phrase can express. If we interrogate God on the question of why he chose the exact form of the world which he did, we can understand his reply just to the extent that our concept of God is at all oriented to this issue. Of course, asking the question of God is itself one way in which the concept is formed, since no view of God ever comes all at once. God's nature filled in as questions are asked and answers are assembled.

To have a "concept" of God means that, with its aid, we are able to answer questions for him. This is not too unlike the function that concepts serve in other situations. To explain the action of a person, we form a concept about his nature in virtue of which his action may be rendered intelligible. We can do the same for God too, and in this sense there is no reason why we should not ask, and he answer, our question, "Why did you do that?" If the ingredients that went into the world did not necessarily involve a choice, our question would be quite different and so would the answer which is given for God.

When we answer for God, "Because I wanted to!" this

points to the element of volition which must enter into the process. On its own, nothing necessitates absolutely one form for creation over another. Thus, without the power of will to decide, no particular form of the world would take shape. Does this mean that we are dealing with a tyrant God, one who dominates others by superior force of will? Not unless will is unrestrained in God or is capable of getting out of control, and we have no evidence that this is the case. What we see is a thoroughly reasoned world; it can be grasped by reason, analyzed mathematically, and partially controlled. Yet, reason alone is not sufficient to account either for the detail of the particular form that emerged or for the exact degree of evil and destruction included.

Even if we take "goodness" to be a complex of criteria with competing and not fully compatible forms, if "good" can be a factor although not one which of itself yields a single direction but only such that it narrows the range of choice—even if this is the case a further element seems required in order to explain the particular form which the world in fact took. "Power" is crucial wherever decision is not automatic, i.e., power to support a conclusion, but will is still involved as a needed ingredient. This is what "Because I wanted to!" means.

A tyrant might not pay attention to reason and to the various criteria for goodness. It is not a tyrannical will which we need to locate in God but only a volition strong enough to explain why he created the world in just this way when he labored under no necessity to do so. Where necessity does not dominate but is itself dependent on decisions which did not have to be, an area of choice remains, and only the power and firmness of will can explain the precise form which the actual choice took. To say this involves a special sense of "to explain," for it does not mean to give an account which sets forth why a certain form had to be fixed without alternative.

When our conduct is not irrational, when it does not ignore standards of value, when our alternatives are narrowed and structured by these processes—then what we must explain is that, by our own choice, we drew a line at one place rather than another within the narrowed spectrum. We acted in one way rather than following another possible route. This is not a tyranny of will; it is simply will's natural function. If criteria are too heterodox to yield a specific route, but if as they are selected they do succeed in narrowing the range, then "will" works within rational limits to yield a definite outcome which otherwise would be impossible.

"Why did he choose to do it in just this way?" is the question to which "Because I wanted to!" is a fitting reply for God to make. What Nietzsche failed to see is that only God, not man, is really beyond good and evil. Our value structure has a certain flexibility and a certain looseness that enables us to substitute one form of value for another, but on the whole its form can only be radically altered more in thought than in fact. In thought we can actually follow God's freedom to form different basic sets of value criteria, but, given his decision for this particular world, our range is now set within good and evil and not above it—except in thought and in any violence which attempts to tear down the structure itself. Given God's reasons to create, i.e., to form a self-sustaining body, to allow knowledge and improvement, it is only a firm will which can account for the precise and detailed form that God's creative will did indeed yield. He must simply have wanted it to be this way.

Mentally we can rehearse God's logic, but this is effective only up to a point. If we try to subtract certain features, e.g., unity, we discover that some form of unity is a necessary condition for creation, but still we do not see why it had to have the exact degree which we find before us. Unity could have bound us much more tightly than it does, just as Plotinus and Spinoza thought. On the other hand, it could hold us less together than it does. The latter alternative would make cooperation even more difficult than it is, but the former would make it more possible, as Spinoza has suggested. We can see the two extremes within which God worked, but this does not tell us why the line was drawn precisely at the point it was so that it yielded the degree of unity within which we live. God seems to follow Aristotle's golden mean in his actions, but a "mean" is a general directive and not a precise determining factor. In addition to this, life would indicate that God actually drew very few lines precisely down the middle. Therefore, the line his finger traced through the infinity of possibles got its general direction from norms which reason can follow, but its precise location can only be derived from the power of will to determine and to hold itself to a decision which is somewhat left of center.

We see God's voluntarism most clearly in any area of defect which man now is able to correct. Why did God refuse to improve what man became able to do? As we have said, the traditional answer points out the value of this struggle for man, but that is at best a partial answer. It is an answer, to be sure, but it is not one that accounts for the precise form which our world took. The Garden of Eden is not the only alternative to what we now have. That kind of idyllic existence might in fact spoil man, but we could learn a lesson of stern self-reliance and hard work and still have circumstances a little more favorable than those which were imposed on us. Conditions are not so bad that we cannot exist and improve, but they might be a little less severe and crushing and still not make man either soft or ununderstanding. One does not have to kill to teach a lesson; God willed a slightly more violent world than any rational criteria alone would dictate.

We need not demand total perfection in the natural order, like a good Swiss watch or a romantic dream, but neither is it necessary that our world have the degree of defectiveness which at times it does. The reason why it does, we can follow up to a point. Whether we should be furious about this unnecessary harshness and reject God because he is more brutal than he need be depends on how we appraise his overall aim and his ultimate intentions. Based on immediate needs, God's course is at present only partially understandable, but it is not at all comprehensible if we think that his aim was to produce the best possible order, since that is not what we have been given to live in. Yet even the Christian interpretation of his ultimate aim and saving action does not justify the precise degree of suffering to which we are now susceptible. After reason has gone as far as it can go, only will can account for the brute fact of the world's unpleasantness.

What do we do in the face of a voluntaristic God? It is so much easier to deal with one whose actions are solely accounted for by reason and some single notion of goodness. If "reason" is not a necessary structure in itself but is merely the power of apprehension applied to both the actual and the possible, then not all the possibles are compossible. In this case reason can discern compatibilities and incompatibilities, but it cannot yield a single course of action on this basis alone. If "good" is seldom singular but has at least several meanings, such criteria can structure and group possibilities, but they cannot determine them to one and only one form. In the face of such a situation, a God capable of decisive will is needed if a resolution is to come about (which it did), but what are we to do now when we are left confronting him? We ask our questions, but the replies that come are only partly rational.

A God who moved to one course of action by a fixed reason would be easier to deal with, but our world is too flexible and it evidences too much contingency for this to be true. It is harder to accept a decision that was not rigidly dictated, and we do have trouble at times accepting our world and our lot. If we can do that, we can accomplish much—at times—within the given framework, but it is not easy for us to accept these conditions as given. In the face of this, is man not allowed to object? Doesn't he have the right of appeal? When all the reasons are given and the range is set so that only God's saying "Because I wanted to!" yields a precise result, can man still dispute this decision and file a protest? It is in the area left open to discrimination that men most often object when their own decisions are disputed. Interestingly enough we have no evidence that God is so touchy, i.e., that he either rejects or resents our protests over the actions of his will as men so often do.

Of course, men are sensitive because their powers are limited, and they know that it may not be possible for them to maintain a decision in the face of adverse criticism. Sensitivity here seems to denote insecurity. God is secure in his infinite power; he can sustain his decision without wavering, and thus he need have no fear of man's protest demonstrations. He does not tremble at the prospect of a divine-human confrontation. We guard our less than necessary decisions with violence in order to cover up the fact that they do not need to be as we have made them. Men occasionally do, but God always does, accept correction silently. Can his will move again at a later time to correct the unnecessary hardships imposed by his earlier decision at the instant of creation?

If God accepts complaints silently, this does not always mean that he acknowledges that he is "wrong" in his decision. Men sometimes are silent as a way of turning back criticism. However, God might be saying though his quietness, "Yes, I know it could be done another way and that this would have certain obvious advantages for men, but I simply did not choose that route." His silence may be telling us to wait and see how it all comes out, or it can even indicate his acceptance of the responsibility for the unnecessary destruction. This is a burden God can take upon himself without breaking under it, something which our guilt-ridden consciences often cannot do. Someone had to make a decision or else we would have had no created order. All that is possible cannot bring itself to actual form. That is too much for a world to bear and too chaotic. The rational application of value standards to all that is possible paves the way, but even that does not draw an exact line. To have any world at all evidences both God's ability to decide, to hold firm to that decision, and to accept the responsibility for its consequences.

If God is not tyrannical, is he nevertheless still "arbitrary" in his action? No, given the degree of order which we do find around us, "arbitrary" is too strong a term to apply. To be arbitrary means to act without reason, and we have asserted that rational standards are adhered to but that they simply are not enough to determine one and only one course of action. Our world has a perfectly rational frame; it just does not have a necessary one. Furthermore, what is arbitrarily arrived at seems equally capable of being changed in the next instant, and our particular created order does not appear to be that insubstantial at its base. Once a process was elected to bring it to its present form, the world remained steady on its course, and this is not what we would expect if confronted by an arbitrary will. To be flexible and variable is not the same as to be arbitrary.

What we appear to face in God's action is a new version of Aristotle's "golden mean." Between what is necessary and what is merely arbitrary we can discover a middle ground. We can see good reason for God to have selected what he did; his action was neither arbitrary nor rigidly determined. The absolute infinity of all that is possible is such that it does not allow necessity to govern creation. What is possible is too large and too varied, and too much of it is incompatible to allow the formation of an actual world to be controlled by strict necessity. However, if God were arbitrary in the face of the vast realm of all that it is possible to create, this would not yield a substantial created order either. God is self-communicating and not selfish, so that he is willing to compromise with possibility in order to create a workable world. He does not simply freeze into inaction as we often do when we face a challenge from outside ourselves. Thus, he has no reason to withhold this attribute of his from creation, i.e., the solidity of substantial existence, but he must avoid both arbitrariness and strict necessity in order to do this.

He could have created a world not based on a substance form of existence, as some philosophers have advocated.[23] Then the beings of the world would not have qualities that belong to their nature of necessity; yet in fact he seems not to have followed that looser model for Being, although these nonsubstance forms of relations do exist in thought and may perfectly well be traced out in various logics. In point of fact, we apparently have had communicated both to us and to the natural order the divine attribute of substantial existence. Our world is not a loose connection of properties. It is a world in process, but it is a process of substances.

Our suggested "golden mean" for God's action is a "new" idea in the sense that this ethical concept has often been connected more strongly with necessity in action than is our intention here. In applying the concept of a mean to ethical behavior, Aristotle wanted to provide for a greater flexibility and variability in conduct than he found possible in his apprehension of the world's physical frame. Still, if the world's order were necessary, the mean in conduct would have to operate within rather strictly defined limits. However, if we do not see necessity as governing the physical form of the world, then God's action in setting nature's limits must also have followed a golden mean. Nevertheless, the alternative norms which will shape this mean are themselves basically more numerous and flexible than Aristotle thought, which means that the selection of a good combination is not at all an obvious matter.

To locate a mean, thus, cannot simply be achieved by rational thought alone and by applying a fixed set of value norms. These delimit a range and climate that obviously had alternatives. But, even then, God seems to have willed a path which is neither quite right down the midpoint nor in conformity with every possible and applicable value standard. He adds the power of his will, and its ability to sustain any decision, to the relevant value norms and rational criteria. This enables him to move to create an order

which is either a little to the right or a little to the left of
a simple golden mean.

In giving the answer for God in this chapter which provides at least some reason for the degree of power which
evil has, we must keep in mind how sharply this differs
from most of the traditional views of God. Our recent experience may require new answers if God is not to be lost
in a wave of violence. However, any contemporary account
of God's actions will become more clear (and perhaps
more forceful) when it is contrasted with how earlier
authors have described God's actions and the reasons for
them. John Hick has given a good account of the variety
of traditional answers to the problem of evil,[24] although it
is interesting to note how little his own account rests upon
any significant change in our conception of God's nature.

Hick really is quite traditional in accepting the world's
structure as given and in confining the problem of evil to
man's moral actions. Admittedly, he "answers" the problem by "eschatology," that is, by seeing evil as defeated in
the end and as "made to serve God's good purposes" (p.
400). Essentially he wants a "universalism" in which all
are saved, but the crucial issue is whether we can in fact
hold God intentionally responsible for heaping evil on us
to a degree greater than necessary for any good purpose.
Hick thinks a final blessedness will render worthwhile "all
the pain and travail and wickedness that has occurred on
the way to it" (p. 376), but to say this is to miss seeing
the voluntary aspect of God's nature and the side of divinity which goes beyond the necessary limits.

Chapter 8

"WHAT A COMEDIAN!"

One answer to the interrogation of God on his plans for this world has been that, whatever the present appearance may be, it will actually come out all right in the end. Many have believed just that. It certainly is a possibility that cannot be denied absolutely, but neither is it a future alternative which can simply be accepted. A "tragedy" is a story which, in its overall sense, ends in destruction whatever its moments of humor and pleasure may have been. A "comedy" need not be funny at every step of the way, but it can be ruled happy in retrospect if its ending is pleasant and if it fulfills rather than destroys desires. To any suggestion that the dramatic scheme intended by God for our world is that of a comedy, our first reply should be, "What a comedian!"

By this reply we mean that, if God's design was to fulfill man (as has been asserted), some of the avenues he has chosen seem less than funny. If God is a comedian in the technical sense of one who has designed a drama with a pleasant outcome, what first impresses us is that his means at times seem needlessly extreme. It is true that, in order to be a comedy, every step need not be a happy one, and all suffering is not excluded. Still, if comedy is the intent, the means which God has chosen seem harsh and

105

strange in many ways. In order to be taught, we do not need to be crushed, so that, even if we expect an ultimately good solution to the world's plan, we still have not explained why the comedy takes such apparently strange and overly severe forms. If the good are restored in the end, this does not take away the fact that they often suffered needlessly in the process.

It is very difficult to understand God as the designer of a comedy, and it is not at all an easy task, since his comedy takes such bizarre forms at times. Everyone is familiar with an intended comedy that assumes strange modes, even given its supposed intent as pleasant. With our human friends, if we are generous and secure enough, we forgive them; but how can we have the strength and the love necessary to forgive God for this mixed enterprise to which he has committed man? Our love is blocked by the fact that this course is not necessary and that it goes too far. In fact, it goes much farther than reason dictates, if God's concern is of the kind that Christians report.

Again, this may, of course, point to God's "testing," since such a factor is familiar enough in human endurance tests, and it is one that many religions do report as true of God's actions toward men. That may explain part of our difficulty, but it is not enough to remove all question. Some trials do test our loyalty, but others break us, and many burdens fall upon those who are completely unequipped to cope with them. Had God neatly apportioned the test to fit the talents and limits of each person to bear them, that would be another matter. As it is, the world he created is not quite that considerate.

In our attempt to explain God's excessive action (not irresponsible or impossible but simply sometimes excessive), several routes are open to us. It may be that the history of

the world as a whole will be written by the last man as
being on the whole a tragedy but still a comedy in parts.
That is, man as a race will cease, his accomplishments
will ultimately crumble or remain with no one to appreci-
ate them; and still, in spots and at times and with certain
individuals in the course of time, the drama can be said to
have had a good short-range ending. That is the summary
as many men have seen it, and certainly it may be true, for
men have achieved great things at times both publicly and
privately. Yet this is a hard conclusion, particularly if one's
base is democratic rather than aristocratic. Why?

To be satisfied with a partial comedy is to be uninter-
ested in the fate of men as a total group. True, most men
are, as a matter of fact, more concerned with the success
of their own group or their ability to create favorable conditions for themselves than they are with any overall appraisal of whether mankind as a whole will have a happy
outcome. Most exceptional accomplishment is aristocratically oriented, or else the achievement of excellence would
not be possible at all. Men simply are not all equal in na-
tive talent, and to ignore the selection of the best is to
court degeneration. To achieve an immediately happy
outcome, whether in terms of personal pleasure or in the
production of a quality product, we must pay attention to
guarding the limits of our life or our group. Yet, outside
those brilliant spots, most men seem deprived and very
few share in these islands of comedy.

God might be an aristocrat, then, who is satisfied to
produce moments of success and a few startling examples
of individual greatness. If so, we do not care if the scheme
as a whole is a tragedy in its oucome as long as comedy
is possible by human effort through a concentration of
resources. That is one view which we can take about God,

but it at least is not the Christian one, and that is why theodicy is such a much more difficult job on a Christian basis. According to the followers of Jesus, God is a democrat who cares for all men alike without distinction while intending a good outcome for everyone as well. In contrast to this leveling outlook, his world is not democratically structured by nature, and its brutalizing aspects are hard to reconcile with this divine intent. Comedy intended for all, not only for the talented and fortunate few—that is an aim not easily seen as evident simply from the way we understand the world and our situation.

In addition to his democratic tendencies, the Christians have announced a God of compassion and passion, and these characteristics are even more difficult to reconcile. For, if he does care about what each one suffers, his concern certainly does not presently appear to be very effective. This is not to say that man alone is not capable of some great acts of compassion and self-sacrifice. Yet these actions often are less characteristic of the religious people of the world than of the secular. In fact, what has blocked many from attributing good intentions to God is the stubborn inhumanity and the minor injustices committed in his name by religious persons. Wherever it may be present, compassion is not evident in the rather blunt and brutal format of the world. It may characterize God's nature, nevertheless, but the point is that this is not unavoidably evident.

Our intent is not so much to make a present evaluation, however, since we have admitted that a different ending can change the picture into a comedy and maybe even into one of democratic proportions. Perhaps all unjustified loss will be restored in the end and every undeserved wrong will be righted. Nevertheless, such an ending is not very apparent now, and assuming God's favor for a democracy rather than an aristocracy only compounds the difficulty. Even granting all this, since the means are more destructive than necessary, it is not clear that even the end will justify the means used.

Even among those who are called "God's people," it is hard to see the comic side of the drama as being unmistakably greater than the tragic. The religious of the world do not appear to fare much better than most, nor is it even clear that they are the most virtuous. History as a sequence of developments has taken certain good turns, but, balanced as a whole, one would be at a loss to see that there is any clear evidence of a totally good outcome. A humanistic outlook can limit its range in this respect, and it is able to consider less than the whole in its evaluation; but theodicy, unfortunately, has the task of balancing the total record of creation.

Given this universal perspective, "comedy" of course still refers only to the eventual outcome. In this case life on earth can be tragic right up until the moment when the loss is recouped, and this can occur at any time before the final curtain. Thus, it remains possible for anyone to believe that God's intervention can accomplish such a feat. The evidence does not totally rule this out, but then neither does it indicate that this is an outcome which can be expected. The outer picture is not decisive, but, if total democracy—not pockets of achievement however great—is to be the standard, the rectifying action is going to have to be quite radical, and we have to admit that the score to date does not indicate very favorable odds. Too many have been born and died in poverty and ignorance—situations deliberately chosen by the same God who must deliver us—to make any such belief in an eventually favorable outcome an unlikely story where the masses are concerned. This pessimistic decision, of course, depends upon accepting only the world as it stands and admitting no other extramundane existence.

Of course, "universalism" need not be assumed. Whatever form it may take, many men seal their own fate for themselves consciously and deliberately. In a world that allows at least limited freedom, no God needs to turn tragedy into comedy either for those who reject him and who work against such general improvements as are possible, or for those who seek merely their own gain to the exclusion of all others. Yet, even if this view is accepted, the world and its history are full of miserable millions who in no such conscious way ever rejected God or any good cause. Their circumstances were not such as even to give them a chance to do so. Unless the group for whom the ultimate end is comic is to be very small, the situation in evaluating the aims of creation really is quite desperate. Given the scale upon which the world was created, a small group of salvaged human beings does not seem to be a very economic goal. That much could have been achieved with less expenditure, so that the scale of the cosmos itself would indicate some larger intent or else none at all.

How, then, is evil, that force which destroys and thwarts fulfillment, to be overcome? We test the means employed, if the intent is said to be the favorable outcome of a comedy, and most of the time it is hard to reconcile an overly harsh system with any asserted compassionate aim. Thus, it is not our problem to consider exactly how evil might be overcome in order to realize this ultimate purpose, but we do need to see that the situation is quite desperate and that the means chosen are not easy to accommodate to the end intended. We do know that, if the intent is democratic (not universal rescue but unrestricted openness of opportunity) vs. limited pockets of human success, the means used to overcome the deteriorating force of evil will also have to be quite drastic. This clearly would involve an extensive modification of nature's present permissive but slightly prejudicial frame.

It may yet all turn out to be a comedy, if given sufficient radical alterations, but still we know that it could have been programmed as a comedy in a slightly lighter vein in the first place. Some comedies are funny, but this particular cosmic drama of ours is so only in isolated moments. Ours is heavy drama, and there is no absolute reason why it could not have been lightened some in mood. True, it is gay and frivolous at times, but its general dramatic form is rather somber. The humor might have been a little clearer and the tragedy a little less pronounced. Some evil can be instructive and act as a purifying purpose, but much serves no such useful purpose. A slight drop in the level of tragedy would prevent no good; in fact, it would make the comedy more easy to discern.

Can any future change, whatever it may be, justify the present situation? It is not at all clear that any good outcome could ever justify the horror of some of the means employed. Even if we admit that part of the horrors in the world are of human origin, still God granted existence to a world within which it is possible for men to sink that low when he might at least have put greater restraints on these degenerative tendencies and damaged freedom not a bit. In fact, by restricting the scope of the evil to which men could sink, he might have increased freedom, since severe injury actually limits our free powers. Furthermore, natural destruction could have been held more within bounds, and this would at least have allowed a greater number of men time to try to develop themselves more fully. Too many are culturally and physically deprived, and their potential never really has a chance to unfold in spite of every effort. Genuine opportunity is given to the very few, so it is a little hard to see how a good surprise ending can relieve the burden placed on God by the excessive means he has employed. Many are likely to feel that, no matter how it turns out in the end, the damage done in the process is not removable by any compensation. Can even a happy ending shift the balance away from a preponderance of tragedy?

It is commonplace in our dealing with men that any damage once done to a person or to a relationship is almost impossible ever to overcome completely. We can never quite restore ourselves to an earlier happier time. At best, a kind of patching up is possible, but things seldom are ever as good as new again once the damage has been done. This means that any comic ending, in order not to be outweighed by the irreparable damage involved, will have to amount to a total restoration of all the damaged parts. We can sometimes renew ourselves and restore our failing health, but the balance of the record is still going to be tragic if such patching up is all that can be done. A kind word at the end simply does not save a situation from being tragic. Extensive damage done in the course of the race is not so easily set right.

If we are to view the drama of man as a comedy, then, in order to do this it will require us to revise our notion of "comedy." Given God's good intent, still the means he employed cannot easily be reconciled as being necessary to achieve his goal, so that the techniques adopted and the circumstances under which we are forced to live exceed the limits required by the goal alone. Once again we come across the notion of a hidden God; for, if his purposes are all-good, it is even less possible in that case to discover this intent by any simple inspection of the present process. Like Kierkegaard's penchant for adopting pseudonyms, God does not immediately appear to be the author of this cosmic play. Given what we are told about his compassion and his goals, it almost looks as if someone else wrote the script for him.

We demand of God to know why he did what he did, and, when we are told that his intent is to produce a comedy, then the sharpness of our question is simply heightened. Not that an answer cannot be given for God, but the revelation of his proposed good intent simply makes it even more difficult to explain his selection of the means. Our notion of comedy will first have to become more complex; and once again we discover that a simple idea of God, e.g., one dominated by unity and love, will not do. If the world's process were a clear expression of this, that would be different; but the strange contrast of this drama, which is billed as a comedy, with the somewhat incongruous means—that requires a more complex God. He must be a being with a balance of forces and factors, one to whom devious routes are not inappropriate. If this be comedy, God certainly makes the most of it.

Freud, as we all know, has another prediction for how the future will develop. He thinks that the human drama can become more of a comedy, but it will do this essentially by giving up primitive superstitions and by freeing itself from religion.[25] We have become moral by internalizing external compulsions, but, in an evolutionary scheme, the question now is whether man is ready to take that function over from religion (p. 14). We turned to religion in earlier times to protect ourselves from a feeling of helplessness against nature, and so we called the forces "father" which threatened us, in order to feel more secure (p. 27). Now, Freud feels, the "scientific spirit" can replace the protection which religion formerly provided (p. 69).

Freud prophesies that religion will be abandoned and that man can deal with the world via science (p. 78). He has his own prediction of what "man come of age" means, and our only advantage over Freud is that we have lived a little farther into the age of modern science. Most certainly, there are many who have abandoned religion for science, but what we do not find to have happened is that the world and man have been made safe from fear through the "scientific spirit." Thus, in considering the possibility of the world drama turning out to be a comedy, we have to ask whether any human achievement to date seems capable of producing that change on a significantly large scale, or whether any radical alteration can still only come from the outside. If so, this requires a God of considerable power and control in order to achieve any general comic effect.

Chapter 9

HOW TO LIVE WITH UNCERTAINTY

Decisions, decisions, decisions! Men who are not "really alive" do not face this persistent problem. They accept their given situation without any attempt at conscious alteration. However, for the creative person and in the eras and the places in which new things are born, decisions govern life, and the men who know how to make them win. Merely to be able to make decisions and to live with them is no guarantee that they will be "right," of course; but at least we must first learn not to retreat in the face of a demand for decisions. Then, once made, the world can evaluate the results of our effort. Where life is active, whether for good or for evil, there we find one decision after another being made. Too often we have taken this as a characteristic of human existence alone and then have described God as beyond the necessity for decision. Now, however, we know that this is a false distinction, no matter how great the other differences between God and man may be.

Our world rests on divine decisions, and it has a base no more nor any less firm than that. A "decision" need not be insubstantial. At its best it actually is that which provides "substance," i.e., the capacity for continued independent (vs. dependent) existence. We make a decision to get married and establish a family, and that decision gives us our independence. Our world does not just simply exist as it is. Existence is conferred on it, or on anything else, only by having some decisions made, since all that is possible is too much and cannot come into existence without specific selection and exclusion. If we can learn to understand those situations which demand decision and to deal with them, we will see that they are not as uncertain as they might at first appear.

The certainty which our world has, therefore, is the degree of certainty which can be attributed to it as the result of a series of decisions. No Broadway musical achieves successful form without a million decisions being made. All of human culture and society rests upon a similar base; and existence of this kind has a solid enough appearance, and it is open to our rational grasp. Decisions need not be arbitrary; good ones depend in turn upon an understanding of that which is possible, and this is the ultimate basis of all existence and understanding.

In order to understand why God acted as he did, it is necessary to make a partial appeal to the divine will. Is this, as Spinoza thought, "the refuge of ignorance"? [26] It will be thought of in this way only if necessity is demanded as a condition for knowledge and, most important, only if the will's action is not based upon reasons. Our whole analysis here has tried to indicate that "will" need not be irrational as it functions in men and that it never is in God. The superabundance of alternatives which we face is such that reason is necessary in order to reach a decision; however, it is not sufficient in itself to determine one and only one outcome for us. Such a theory as this is not a refuge of ignorance. It is merely a recognition that possibilities, although they can be reduced, in the most important situations cannot be cut down to only one set by rational thought alone. Reasons can be given for such selective action, but they are not the total explanation.

Ignorance does remain in the sense that, both for men and for God in the most crucial choices, reasons can be given only within a certain range. Beyond that, we find an area which must be left to decision. Although we can see the advantages and disadvantages of each situation according to a variety of value criteria, as we have already noted, we often cannot say why the line was drawn precisely where it was except that the power of will drew it at that point. We acknowledge the fact of the precise form of the resulting decision, but that is not to say why it could not have been "a little more to the right or a little further to the left." In trying to understand God, we may often be confused by man's sometimes ignorant choices. God never acts in ignorance, but our blindness concerns the precise form that will's decision takes after reason has completed its analysis.

Whenever we act in ignorance, we often do harm unintentionally. This is an ignorance which could have been eliminated, so that, in deciding to obscure man's mode of knowledge unless it is corrected with great effort, God doomed man to commit more harm than necessary. Of course, some men do damage intentionally and with the clear aid of knowledge, but much havoc also results simply because our vision is more limited than it needs to be. We would like to be better than our halting intelligence and our fumbling intentions allow. God never acts in this way, but he did act to set the conditions for the less-than-ideal type of action open to us. Why he did not increase our range of knowledge slightly in order to relieve unintentional suffering—that we cannot say. His will did not act in that way, to put it simply. We are not ignorant of the consequences of alternative ways, but finally we come up against the hard fact of will, i.e., that the exact form we have is the result of God's specific decision.

Can we learn to live with this and with the element of uncertainty which it involves? Before we can do this, a lesson in obedience, discipline, and acceptance is required. This does not mean that we can neither question nor demand answers. We can and we do. But it does mean that we must begin by accepting the decision handed to us that outlines our limits; we take it as our starting point without being able to explain beyond a certain point why it is that way. The only unequivocal necessity is that some decision be made. Men often get furious when their decisions are questioned. God is not so insecure. We can and should question the choices he has made, but this does not get around the fact that we must first accept it as the context which is simply given to us for our divine discussion.

The kind of world we have sketched has an element of uncertainty at its very base. Can we learn to live within it? Certainly this fact does not mean that nothing can be achieved. Our actual achievements in art and science deny this. What it does mean is that achievements, if they are not accidents as some are, must be based on a grasp of the elements of uncertainty and then on a mastery of them. The structures which we build, whether intellectual or economic or political, all incorporate both that element of uncertainty and the basic necessity for reaching a decision—or else they are not stable. We can learn to live with uncertainty but not if we try to reduce it to some form of certainty. We may impose a form of certainty on the world for a moment—whether in philosophical theory or in structuring society—but the constant shift of the human scene soon demonstrates the falsity of such a premise by refusing to be stopped at that point. We can live with uncertainty but only by appraising its degree and then by accepting this as the basis for as firm a decision as is possible in those circumstances.

We can and should go farther than this when we interrogate God. We can ask why he preferred such a degree of uncertainty when he could have imposed absolute necessity on the world's order. The first answer God might give is that to have done so would mean to have eliminated any area for human freedom. This reply will be considered in more detail in the next chapter. For the moment it is sufficient to note that this is not a complete answer, since we are faced with more uncertainty than freedom demands as its condition. Our question must go beyond that and ask why he preferred just the degree of uncertainty which he did, no more and no less. To deal with uncertainty does reflect God's own situation, and yet, *in opening man to this indeterminiteness, God placed burdens upon him which man is less equipped to bear than God*. We can see why to create some uncertainty is a more honest world for God than one without it. Nevertheless, this still leaves open the question regarding the precise degree of uncertainty, which is not fully explained, and the question of why God should be less fair to man than to himself in the conditions which he imposes.

If we can see why God might prefer a system with some degree of uncertainty in it without being able to give a specific reason for the exact degree decided upon, then at least the range we are working within becomes clear. Too little uncertainty would not be an honest world and would restrict freedom; too much would paralyze man's powers and make accomplishment either rare or impossible.

Within that range God's will moved in its decision at the instant of creation, neither irrationally nor in such a way that we are ignorant of its basic rationale but so that the precise form of the decision could not be predicted in advance of the decisive action which finally fixed it and the power which holds it in place. Looking back, we can trace the route and the degree which were selected, and this is why history can take on the aspect of certainty. But such definitive accounts are possible only in retrospect as the result of the decisions taken; they cannot be given in advance of them.

Once made, what kind of certainty does a decision have, or what kind of certainty can be based upon it? In God's case a universe is built upon it. We can be sure that these are the forms and the laws which he assigned, but we cannot be certain that they are the only possible ones. Here the power and consistency of the decider is the key factor. Not all is possible within God's nature, and yet nothing outside God opposes any consistent choice, Since his power is unlimited, he can sustain his choice without reversal. Reason cannot persuade him to alter his decision, because his choice was first made by the aid and within the limits of reason. Another alternative may also be quite rational, but reason alone cannot induce God to alter a decision, once it has been enacted by reason's aid, merely to adopt another reasonable alternative form. He cannot afford to be as capricious as we are; worlds depend on him to maintain their consistency.

The certainty that men's decisions have will vary quite considerably from this divine firmness. Without rejecting the basic framework once it is established, God may alter his will to work within that framework or even to alter the framework itself, if this does not amount to a complete rejection of it. Since God made a firm decision and is fully capable of sustaining it, we can predict that such a reaction would be rare, but, nevertheless, it certainly is both possible and conceivable. Men, on the other hand, only sometimes calculate the situation and their strength properly. Rarely are they able to sustain their decisions without basic alteration, although often this can be done if needed modifications are continually supplied. Because their knowledge and grasp is limited, men seldom do achieve this divine degree of firmness as a result of their decisions, but it is not impossible. Our most gifted decisions do have this sustaining and adaptable power. Whatever we come to call "classical" partakes of this solidity.

Most men will at sometime overreach either their knowledge or their capacity or both, and then any certainty is likely to be disappointing if it depends on that decision. Desperate and destructive effort often is poured out in an attempt to sustain a human decision which is poorly grounded, but this is an extreme to which God is never forced. Men are also capable of giving their words and their decisions the appearance of infallibility, so that, by the arguments given, one would think that we might rest certainty upon some human decision. A few such decisions may in fact be very close to the maximum certainty which man can achieve within a world itself based upon uncertainty, but all certainty is always a matter of degree where the decisions of men are concerned. It would be strange indeed if men were capable of a greater degree of certainty than God has allowed to himself.

To learn how to appraise the degree of certainty which we can recognize in the result of any human decision—this tests our skill as men in an uncertain world. To place too little or too much certainty on any particular human thought or enterprise is to fail to find the basis upon which alone human construction is possible. As to basic principles, most men tend to be blind and to accept as certain decisions announced with an air of authority. The rebels and the men of creative insight are those who can sense the degree of flexibility lying at the base of all existing decisions; one will then use this insight to destroy while the other will employ his sensitivity to build a new basic framework that makes advance possible.

A "metaphysical instinct" is one which senses that the substance of the world is made of decisions. Aristotle thought that the substance of the world had to be based on necessity. Now we discover that we do have a substantial form of existence but that its origin is less than necessary. Actuality is achieved as the result of decisions; it is the stuff of which existence is made. To discover this and to learn how to handle it is to have insight into Being's structure and to develop power over it and the nonbeing which always threatens it. Decisions, of course, can only operate on something, and this means upon the full extent of the possibles, i.e., the unlimited range open to God's view or the more limited range which he has set out for man.

Occasionally our gaze becomes fixed upon a set of possibles that are not quite those of our world and yet that are not completely outside its structure. In this case a decision or a theory is hard to sustain, and it will tend to be successful just to the degree that the possibles used as a base are similar or dissimilar to those which are actually ingredient in our world. As a matter of fact, most theories and most decisions are probably based on insight that is "a near-miss"; very few rest on a perfect grasp of our world's specific structure or on the exact makeup of our situation. Words and concepts make it hard to grasp actuality directly and yet easy to settle for a close possibility.

How can we live with uncertainty? How does God do it? The answer: By not acting beyond his power to enact or to sustain (e.g., by not trying to give power to possibles that are not compossible), by not pretending that a completed decision is necessary when it is so only to a degree, by accepting responsibility for decisions made, and by working within the framework selected rather than constantly referring to and yearning for some form which was excluded by an earlier decision as henceforth impossible. For man, however, to reverse a decision once made is not always bad, especially when it means either obtaining a more accurate grasp or the realization of a new value. This is difficult to do if men pretend that their decisions are either necessary or are the only possible ones. Thus, to learn to live with the uncertainty of decisions is the first condition for human improvement, and our failure to do this is responsible for the inflexibility which so often blocks progressive change.

The world could have been less certain in its rules and in its structure than it is, or it could be even more certain. To recognize where the flexibility does and does not lie is man's most prized insight. To fail to see when things need not be as they are—this is the source of man's great inhumanity to himself and to others. If we grasp this situation correctly, in what sense does it help us to answer our question, "Why did you do that?" The first reply is that all coming-into-existence requires some action beyond reason's ability to select. The second is that God has the power to set the limits, within reason's range, at the exact point that he wants to, and he has the ability to sustain existence there. Inside this basic uncertainty, God has agreed with himself to live; men may either rebel and ultimately break themselves and others, or else they can discern these limits and enhance existence by the skillful use of that insight.

In his famous essay *The Rebel,* Albert Camus defines "metaphysical rebellion" as man's "objection to the conditions in which he finds himself as a man." [27] Man protests against his condition and against the whole of creation. This rebellion is a claim "against the suffering of life and death and a protest against the human condition both for its incompleteness, thanks to death, and its wastefulness, thanks to evil" (p. 24). Thus, Camus finds evil in the world to be the center of man's problem and the focal point for his protest and, ultimately, his rebellion. This revolt has the benefit of unifying the men who find themselves leagued in protest. Men discover their solidarity against evil, and, of course, Camus finds that "any concept of superior existence is contradictory, to say the least" (p. 25).

All around the world today men are uniting in protest and rebellion against the inferior conditions granted to them. Camus would like to question a personal God about these initial injustices, but he finds only silence as his answer. In such a desperate situation of worldwide human rebellion seeking to free itself from unfavorable conditions, some attempt ought to be made to see what God's reply might be like today, given our new situation of insight into the desperateness of the human condition when viewed democratically and not aristocratically. Where Camus could not, can we construct a view of a God who can speak out in answer to the protests against him? The conditions that are given to us cause men to rebel today. What kind of God can we discover who would knowingly create conditions so conducive to widespread rebellion?

Chapter 10

WHAT PRICE FREEDOM?

It has been said, but it is a too-easy solution, that all of evil is due to man's freedom and his misuse of it in the sin of defying God. To argue this way is to let God off too quickly, for this explanation attempts to account for evil's presence in our world as a necessity that must be present if men are to be given freedom. Our choice, so the argument runs, is between having freedom, together with the resulting possibility for sin and destruction, and not having freedom at all. In the face of such an alternative, God is pictured as magnanimously granting men freedom in spite of the evil which they will inflict upon themselves. Like most theories which tend to be repeated continually, there is of course an element of truth here. If God had not left men free, certainly the world could have been arranged to be a much nicer place. Unfortunately, such arguments have also tended to be associated with theories of God's foreordination, so that in the end it is not man who plots his sin but God who arranges for him to do so from eternity.

If we eliminate both foreordination and predestination, can it still be argued that evil is the price of freedom? If man is set free from divine determination, can this be achieved only at the cost of allowing evil into this world?

125

One way to begin to answer these questions is to ask
whether all of the faults of the world can be attributed to
man's free action so that they could not be eliminated
unless his freedom were removed? Here the answer in
general seems clearly to be "no," but it involves a matter
of degree. First, there certainly are many natural evils
which men are not responsible for, earthquake, fire, flood,
and plague. It is true that, in his freedom, man may learn
to protect himself partially, but this is still a long way
from accounting for the range and the depth of nature's
destructive forces. Some natural fury can be explained as
having a beneficial chastening effect upon man, but still
natural destruction exceeds the limits required for that.
God clearly must be held accountable for those evils
which are not of human origin, and the dispensing of
justice is not all that is involved here, since nature's evils
rain upon the just and the unjust alike.

Secondly, the matter of degree is perhaps the most per-
plexing fact. Some men do invite destruction through their
voluntary negligence. Others are purified and not destroyed by natural adversity because they have freely
shaped their lives to withstand it, while others are undone
because their bluff of playing fast and loose with life is
called by some disaster. Yet, the degree of natural destruction still could have been lessened. Man could have been
made naturally more immune to physical ills and every
good effect of natural violence would still have been
achieved. Where human evils are concerned, the main
question is one of degree also. Our choice is not between
freedom with evil or safety with no freedom at all. God's
options are wider than that, and, simply for the sake of
achieving an easy answer, men should not try to restrict
God to too simple an alternative.

In point of fact, freedom might have been granted and a few more helpful limits could still have been set. Knowledge, power, and freedom might have been balanced in somewhat better proportions. Education need not be quite so difficult or involve so many obstacles, and still freedom could be achieved. Even where some restrictions on freedom are involved, we live at the end of an era in which men have struggled violently and even destructively to achieve freedom. At the same time millions of others have been perfectly willing to subordinate freedom to a dictatorship (or to an assured income) in order to achieve security and some social improvement. We cannot assume that human freedom is worth any price. It need not cost us quite so much evil to possess it, and to many men some values are apparently worth even more than freedom.

Our question is, What part of the responsibility for the evil and for the undesirable features of our world must human freedom bear? If we are to be able to accept freely, we must also be able to reject, and thus men are capable of negativity. Negativity is an attitude that expresses freedom in men, but it can become corrosive and destructive. This is one price we have to pay for freedom, and yet most of us are ill-equipped by nature to cope with this. The physical odds against us often are too high, so that our situation could have been more favorably constructed than it is. If the resources of nature were more evenly distributed and more readily available, men would not be so willing to sacrifice their freedom for a little bread. What would it have cost God to make the earth's surface a little more fruitful, and what good does he gain by allowing famine? The odds need not have been put so high against freedom, although some built-in pressure away from freedom is probably necessary for its existence and appreciation. To be free one must have the alternative to bind himself; freedom is realized only through the effort to create it or to prevent its loss.

Man bears some responsibility for the unpleasant features of the world as the necessary price for his freedom. However, in the context in which freedom is exercised, in the evil which is not due to freedom, in the extremes which have been made more unfavorable than necessary, it seems that God's share of the responsibility is considerably larger than man's. If God had no alternatives in creating, no alternative structures equally within his range of rational choice, then he is not free, and certainly man would not be so selfish as to demand freedom for himself while denying God his range of choice. Still, God went farther in arranging creation than can ever be accounted for by any necessity to demonstrate his freedom. God seems to have forced man to pay for his (God's) freedom by a higher price than necessary. In the face of these harsh conditions, many men are willing to give up both their freedom and God's.

To find a cause for evil we will have to go farther than freedom, since its conditions require perhaps some but not all of what we experience. Yet in a profounder sense, freedom can explain the extent of evil which is present, because we find that God was free to build a world structured on a free system or not to do so. Given this basic alternative, we learn a deeper meaning of freedom. God was free to go farther than the goal of freedom alone necessitated. It is not so much that his decisions are not governed by value criteria and rational considerations, but that he is capable of stopping short or of going beyond these limits. And so are men. If every man went just as far as his objectives demanded and never stopped short or exceeded them, our life would be considerably different both for good and for ill.

This ability to fall short of, or to go beyond, rational standards—this "freedom-plus" is what God granted to man as a counterpart of his own excessive freedom. We might wish that God had not overstepped the limits required to achieve his end (e.g., freedom), but in that case he surely would not have allowed men to be excessive. For both God and man this possibility to exceed necessary limits, as it was actualized in Being, is the source of the world's great goods and ills. If men did only what was required, much generosity would be missing. However, often they also fail even to do what the given standards demand, and they exceed bounds in violence and horror as well as in love and generosity. The range need not be as wide as it is, and yet it does seem that *both God and man must be free to be excessively bad if they are to be free to exceed love's demand.*

What bothers us is that freedom could be secured and still be less destructive. At their very best men have managed to achieve this difficult combination. We know that God could have imposed this happier framework more widely, but he did not choose to do so. He made it possible for men to be free and to share their liberty with others rather than to destroy them, but this happens only in comparatively favorable circumstances and only for the few and not for the majority. Why did God condemn by unfavorable circumstances so few to be free without being destructive, whether this is as nations or as individuals? If they are not able to achieve this golden mean in freedom, many will reject freedom for security. Freedom's price is often too high, and we are willing to trade it for something less dangerous or more widely applicable to more men. Why was freedom made so dangerous, when it could have been more tightly contained and thus made more successful? And does this excessiveness really teach us anything?

It at least teaches us that God is capable of going beyond the requirements of any goal. He must not be Aristotle's virtuous man who always acts to define a mean. He created a world of extremes in which it was possible for a very few fortunate men to achieve a golden mean of conduct. Yet, in his own creative activity, God has gone farther than any balance of factors required him to do and, if he has not quite acted impossibly in allowing violence, at least he has been excessive. If they had been asked before creation, men would probably have voted for a free system, and God is capable of assuming the limitations on his power and knowledge which are necessary in order to grant this. He has charged us a higher price for freedom than he had to, even if we grant that freedom always requires some accompanying difficulties. *To solve the puzzle of freedom means to solve God's excessive action in creation.*

We criticize God just as we criticize men for going farther than necessary. Men often cannot restore the damage caused by their excesses. Can God? Freedom may be taken as a divine goal, since we have a system in which it is at least possible to be free, although it is difficult to achieve and many are denied even the opportunity. Yet God must also have a motive ulterior to that of opening freedom as a possibility, since his selection in creation went much farther than necessary for that purpose. What can we say about God's possible ulterior aims? What can we discover about God's final intention that might explain why he gave us so much less than ideal conditions for freedom and why in fact he made the conditions under which we live, if not impossible, at least more extreme than necessary? What we can conclude is that he must have aims which are even more basic than freedom, although he evidently did care enough about freedom to make it at least possible for us to achieve it at times. One ulterior motive of God's must be to let us experience the full power of the forces of destruction as he knows them, even to the point of death.

To allow men to be free must be for God a means rather than an end, or else he could have achieved that end more economically and more fully than the system which he chose allows. Can freedom in God give us any clues as to what his aims beyond freedom for man might be? We know that God cannot simply be free, for all that is possible cannot come into existence without producing chaos and a monster universe. He must deny some legitimate claims on existence and hold back some possibilities, although only what comes to exist in fact has feelings which deserve to be considered in the matter. The ignorance of nonexistence is bliss. Were men too easily free, their world would not reflect the depths of the divine problem of dealing with nonbeing. This desire to reflect nonbeing within the world's actual structure can give a better account of God's excessiveness than can the appeal to simply a desire to grant freedom in itself. He deals with destructive forces constantly; man must too or else his impressions of God and Being would be false.

Freedom in that sense is a byproduct of the desire to open the range of Being to the full extent of the possibles rather than to restrict it any further than it already must be. Even so, we sometimes experience more violence from various possibles as they compete for existence than we would like to, but any less conflict would give us a very distorted and too romantic a view of the depths of the divine life and of God's own internal problems. God does not lose control nor is he destroyed in facing this chaotic range, and that is a rather large difference between him and us. For what purpose, then, did God open us to destruction when we might have been more protected? The problem of freedom seems to dissolve into asking why God allowed destruction to have as wide a range as it has. Even if we grant that terror is not always out of hand, what did he hope to accomplish by unleashing this power?

We have returned once more to our original question, "Why did you do that?" What partial answer can our analysis of freedom provide? We began with three divine scandals: (1) Kierkegaard's scandal of the divine becoming human, (2) the Christian assertion that God is a democrat who likes the lowly as well as the gifted, and (3) our own newly uncovered scandal of making God account for why he created a world not as good as possible and more destructive than necessary. What did God have to gain by making the odds against our success so great? This might argue that he is an unfair God, or that he is jealous of his position and thus deliberately makes human competition difficult. This might be; but if, on the other hand, he is a loving and a generous God, the scandal of the world he chose only deepens—unless we can discover some ulterior reason in the apparent madness of his excessive world. The fact that we have sometimes been granted freedom does not actually lessen the scandal in which man has caught God but instead only increases it.

The better we assert God's intentions to be, the more difficult it is to account for the exaggerated means selected.

The Christian paradox is not simply that the divine became human at a point in time. The possibilities for that depend on the kind of view of God and man which you hold. *The Christian paradox involves the reconciliation of God's asserted democratic and generous motives with the considerably less than clear and ideal means which he employed in creation.* His love seems to be a strange one, given the suffering he imposed that goes beyond either the bounds of education or the gift of freedom. Men are willing to pay for freedom, but, as their modern preference for security indicates, they will reject it if the price is too high for the benefits received. We might have accepted Spinoza's fully determined world gladly, if only God had consulted us about creation beforehand.

God must be strong enough not to take an obivous course. He is able to accomplish his purpose with either inadequate or excessive means—which is the kind of bravado, daredevil tactics we sometimes admire in men. He does not require any assistance in this, and he must be so well able to cope with failure that he does not need to take a safe course. A completely serious God would take the standard prescribed course, but the God we are dealing with seems capable of the kind of looseness involved in playful conduct.

This discovery might lead us to a horrifying God, but, on the other hand, can this world still be seen as a creative act of unselfish love? Depending on the end written to the drama, it might be; we have not come to that act yet, however much we may have heard about it. Fortunately, we appear to be up against a God who need not fail in his freedom to try a more difficult feat than necessary. His nerve and power supply are apparently inexhaustible. Our hard questions center more around the unusual meaning of his "goodness" rather than about the degree of his power and control.

When Sartre considers man's freedom as against God's action, he is convinced that "if God exists, man is nothing; if man exists . . ." [28] Thus, Sartre is quite willing to abandon God as the price for man's freedom. In fact, he is convinced that God must go if man is ever to assert his freedom. Sartre is aware of evil in the world, yet he does not so much see it as the result of granting men freedom as he does as the effect of men being bound by their belief in God. Yet today atheism is quite widespread, and so we have to ask whether in fact men seem any more humanitarian and whether evil is any less now that God is gone. In fact, the systematic atheists of our time, the Marxists, seem very good at holding down freedom in the name of a promised future state, and the role of the devil has been played by their disciples at least as many times as by priests.

Must we do away with God in order to discover human freedom, or, if we are to have God, is there a God capable of allowing freedom without hiding behind evil as its supposed price? In considering our modern freedom, it might be possible to find such a contemporary God. Sartre and existentialism have stressed the necessity for human acceptance of responsibility, and we have learned to live in an existential age. With this in mind, we ought to be able to conceive of God as also accepting the responsibility for the results of his own deliberate choices. At the same time, he should allow us human freedom without demanding that man accept the sole responsibility for all evil.

Chapter 11

NOT SO ORIGINAL SIN

In more optimistic days it seemed as if we could no longer accept the idea of original sin. That man has defects which he cannot himself overcome is a hard doctrine to accept if one is really convinced of man's limitless ability to improve himself. Recently, however, existentialism has created an atmosphere conducive to a traditional belief in human sin, and in many quarters there is a renewed receptivity to the concept of "original sin." Although we have the Biblical story of Adam and Eve, there never has been only one view of what "sin" involves. In order to make the idea of original sin meaningful, a contemporary reinterpretation is always needed. In this essay on theodicy, it is not our aim to review the various interpretations of sin or to try to give "sin" a full exposition. But the idea of original sin does raise questions for theodicy, and, in this divine interrogation, there are some issues regarding sin which need to be taken up with God.

First, we want to know: Why was sin incorporated into the world? Since it is each man who sins, each must learn for himself whether his sin is against man or God. But it is God who designed the situation in which we find ourselves, and it need not have been this way. Sometimes it is said that man has to be free to fail in order to be free,

135

so that sin is necessary in order to have freedom. We have just argued in the preceding chapter that, while it is true that some human failure could not be eliminated without restricting freedom, still that is not true of all sin. It is this matter of degree, then, which we want to take up with God in questioning him. It simply is not the case that man could not be free if the situation were designed so that less sin were possible. Freedom is never an absolute quantity. Severe rigidity would make any free act impossible, but we could have been allowed some flexibility for action and still not be capable of the amount of sin which we do.

Sin means to commit a wrong against another human being or to break God's commands as we see them. This may involve either unjustified pride or a refusal to believe and trust when that risk should be taken. Human moral standards vary, so that although every man breaks some code which he feels obliged to keep, the standards themselves are subject to some variation. Insofar as we understand God, we sometimes fail to comply with his demands, but there are also occasions when we are not sure what God intends. God might have created moral and value standards in a more unified and clearly defined set. We sometimes err because the situation is complex and because more than one standard is involved, or we may fail because the context is slightly confused. For our failure we must accept responsibility; but, for creating the unclear situation in which we must act and for the sin resulting from this indigenous confusion, God must take the majority of the blame.

Ignorance is often a cause of sin. God did elect to give us a mental process capable of brilliance, but it is also a mind subject to blindness and one not easy to educate. Some blindness is self-imposed; we simply refuse to see, but there also are many who are not responsible for their ignorance. God could have arranged to distribute intelligence more widely and more evenly and to disseminate understanding more quickly and easily. What would it cost him to eliminate hereditary ignorance and stupidity? Had he elected to do this, humanity as a group certainly would have been in a superior position as far as our ability to refrain from such error as is due to simple ignorance or confusion. We were not given odds as favorable to remaining free from sin as we might have been, so that, to the extent that our situation is less favorable than it could be, God and not man is responsible for the resultant sin.

To be free we must be free to fail, but, had we been better equipped and had the situation been more favorable, our ability to refrain would be greater than it is. Not always but often we do not intend to fall, but our strength is not sufficient to hold us back. For the misuse or the failure of such strength as we have, we can be held accountable; but, for the decision not to provide us with greater powers of resistance and for creating situations too overwhelming for us to withstand—that part of sin becomes God's share. For the imprecisions, the multiplicity of standards, the insufficient level of knowledge and human power—for all of these God assumed responsibility in forming the pattern for our creation. Beyond that, of course, man fails to do what he admits he should do, and for that he cannot shift the blame to God's less than perfect design.

Does he cause us to sin, make escape impossible, and then condemn us for it?—that is the harshest form which our question addressed to God can take. Much transgression seems to come through a blindness or a stupidity and a weakness that is inborn in the situation. We often would

do good and cannot. Sometimes our will has been immo-
bilized by our own previous action, and for that we are
responsible. But at other times the power given to us is
not equal to what we would like to do. Our grasp may
exceed our power, and this imbalance need not exist if
God had chosen to balance things more evenly. In the
area over which they have discretion, men ought to accept
responsibility; but, for the situations which contain less
than optimum conditions, the error here is of God's own
design. For the failure to accomplish the good that we
would do, Paul should have allotted God his share of the
responsibility too.

Our problem is to make an accurate estimate: What
share of the blame for human failure ought man to accept,
and what share must God admit to be due to the unfavorable conditions which he created for us? Were we given
optimum conditions and greater control, we might have
done better, although it is true that we also could have
done worse. That is, sometimes it is clear that the combination of a situation plus his limitations are too much
for a person; but on the other hand, we see that greater
knowledge and power and clarity are in themselves no
guarantee of right action. Greater power can cause even
greater destruction. If conditions were better, some helpless victims might be saved from enforced error, but increased power and knowledge do not in themselves necessarily lead to greater good.

Still, if God had created optimum conditions for us, he
would at least have freed himself from the responsibility
for creating inferior conditions. Then all the blame could
rest on us for the deliberate misuse of adequate tools. Not
having elected that path, God appears to have been willing to accept his share of guilt and to have made himself

a party to man's crimes by incorporating an area of ambiguity. In accepting his share of responsibility for that degree of error which he made it impossible to prevent, God appears to have wanted to participate in this sometimes bloody human drama. He accepts his share of sin, when he certainly could have avoided it, by placing us in blameless conditions. Of course, he can accept this burden without breaking under it, whereas we often find it intolerable to bear.

Kierkegaard outlined a modern reinterpretation of original sin in his *Concept of Dread*.[29] These psychological deliberations attempt to fathom the real possibility of sin and not to treat it as a dogmatic concept. S.K. uses the traditional story of Adam, but he sees in Adam an illustration of what every man goes through. In this sense, every man starts as if we were at the beginning of history as Adam was. Since sin is a loss of innocence we must become capable of sin, and yet one can only become wise in the world by getting rid of innocence. (Is this the reason for God's restriction against eating the fruit of the tree of knowledge?) We must know life's sad facts in order to understand existence, but this loss of innocence only opens each man to the possibility for sin. Innocence is ignorance, and in that state one does not sin. You can harm without knowing it, but that is not sin, since a consciousness of the action is required. Kierkegaard then goes on to account for the loss of innocence through the power of dread which is produced by an awareness of our freedom before it is exercised.

Innocence falls when it faces the nothingness of ignorance and the dread produced by an awareness of our as yet unspecified freedom. We actually fall from innocence in dread of the results of our free actions which are as yet undone. This occurs inwardly in the cowardly person and it renders him capable of sin, so that the story of Adam simply represents this inward fact as an outward event. We read Adam's story, but how sin comes into the world each man understands in himself alone by reflecting on the moment when he first became aware of the results of his free actions and of his responsibility for them. Dread is the dizziness of freedom looking down into all that is possible and open to our action. If at that moment one cannot sustain himself, he succumbs. And the cycle continues, since the dread of sin also produces sin. Small mistakes can multiply and throw a whole life into confusion. However, sin becomes serious when we are finally turned around and find ourselves locked into a radically wrong orientation. Dread is often produced, not so much over the past, but in relation to the future and its possibilities which demand the risk of action.

Without going farther into Kierkegaard's reinterpretation of original sin, it is clear that his psychological analysis is one way to make the traditional doctrine of Adam's fall meaningful once again. It is the internal makeup of each man that is represented in Adam. An analysis like this can explain the disposition of each man to fall, but what it does not explain is why God first set the limits on our powers of resistance just where he did. If our power were greater, it is also true that the pressures could be higher, and this would amount to the same situation. But still, the whole system could have been arranged in a greater harmony of power and pressure; as it is, the balance is more against us than it might be. Our situation isn't hopeless; it is just more difficult than it need be.

Even if we accept S.K.'s modern analysis of the psychological origins of dread in the awareness of freedom and its tendency to make one lose his balance, we are still left with a problem over the fact that we were given a rather fragile and delicate psychological apparatus. This does not mean that we should wish for less sensitivity and awareness. As Kierkegaard says, innocence is not a state one ought to wish to return to. We could be as sensitive as we are, although some men are too insensitive, and still we could have minds which are a little stronger than they are, a little less likely to break and to split apart.

Sometimes dread paralyzes action or causes us to sin in a panic over our freedom in relation to the future and its possibilities. To the extent that we have the power to resist this and to act, we cause ourselves to fall. To the extent that what is demanded is too much for us, it is God's creation of such a situation that must be held accountable, and it is very hard to draw a neat line through these two areas of responsibility. Why God chose not to build us a slightly stronger psychological apparatus and to proportion it better in relation to the forces which it must face—that is the question about sin which God has yet to answer.

In contrast to the usual accounts, sin is "not so original" because the first fall is not a single historical event located at one point. Instead, it is a psychological process through which each man must go. Somewhat ironically, the only sense in which there is "original sin" is that God built some causes or inducements to sin into his creation by virtue of his less than optimum design. In God's first choice, all men were forced to sin when the conditions which later would lead us to it were established. God, not Adam, must now represent original sin due to the precarious situation in which we were placed; at times we are not even supplied with an adequate defense.

Nevertheless, in addition to man's sin which stems from God's original action, men also sin in Adam to the extent that Adam represents that share of the burden which man must still bear for himself. This concerns our failure in a situation in which man's knowledge and his power are sufficient but in which our will is either ineffective or else wrongly oriented. The process which Adam went through, this each man repeats psychologically in his own day. The original conditions for sin are the only guilt which is inherited, and God must bear the responsibility for this from generation to generation.

Had God designed a situation in which man had no one to blame but himself, our relationship to God would certainly be less confused. If we had no reason for complaint against God, the exact degree of our own responsibility would certainly be much clearer. As it is, the mixed situation in which we are forced to live constantly leads men to try to shift the responsibility for their failures to others. It is very likely true that in most instances the defects and the imbalances which were built into the situation are probably only partly responsible for our failures, but this still makes the determination of man's share much more difficult than it might be in some more neatly divided created order. This is an interesting test of man, it is true, since a clouded situation does give him a chance to escape. It is fascinating to see who will openly claim his own share of the blame and who will try to shift everything off to other men or to God whenever his responsibility is not total but only partial.

At this point we come across the divine scandal again, i.e., that, for some some sources of sin, God himself is responsible in his less than perfectly clear design of creation. In interrogating God on this matter, our problem is

to try to see why he did that. In the short run it is true
that, in dividing responsibility between man and God,
when God is silent about claiming his share, this puts an
interesting test upon man not to try to shift responsibility
but to claim his own burden anyway. In a world more
conducive to our success or in a creation without faults,
there would be no chance of avoiding responsibility.
Adam's situation in Eden is pictured in this way, but all
that really teaches us is that God elected not to create an
Eden for us when he very well might have. This divine
decision not to launch man in perfect conditions is more
interesting, but it is also more difficult and harder to appraise than the kind of firmness and certainty that drove
Adam from his Eden. Perhaps Adam accepted too much
responsibility too quickly and should have protested God's
quick judgment.

We do not start in a paradise, and, because of this,
man's share of responsibility is not as easy to appraise.
Where sin is concerned, God and man are partners; God
is silently capable of bearing his part, but man sometimes
breaks under his burden. Some men accept less responsibility than they should, others more, but this would not
happen if God had not left the lines of responsibility so
vague. What we can do and do not do, that we are responsible for. However, we are often also asked to do the
impossible, and, for the extent of the failure which is
beyond our power, this we take to be of God's design.

In this way we are now open to comprehend God's own
problems with himself in creating; but, given a burden
that goes beyond our capacity and that crushes us, what
does God intend to do about that original fault, i.e., about
his own sin? It may still be true in one sense that Jesus
lived without sin, but in another sense it is true that God

as his Father does not. Although we must be careful about judging God by simple and crude human standards, when in the course of developing a concept of God in response to evil we come to the question of sin and responsibility, we must still be ready to assign to God what seems undeniably to be his share. Man ultimately can discover what part he must accept by learning to separate out from the world's evils those which God freely elected in his original choice. Where sin and evil are concerned, we must render unto man what is man's and unto God what is his own.

In trying to understand the origin of evil, Martin Buber finds the Biblical story of the first murder a helpful setting.[30] Of course, Buber believes that an understanding of such a fundamental fact about our world as evil can only come to us with the aid of such stories and myths (p. 115). Myths "tell us of the human constitution and movement of evil" (p. 116), and in this sense myths are true. They embody the experience of man's encounter with evil, and to that extent they are necessary to our understanding. Furthermore, it is clear that Buber accepts such mythical accounts of the origin of evil not so much as a literal account of original sin as a figurative representation of what takes place within the soul (p. 89).

In this case, what we need to study is the account of original sin, for only here will we find a vivid enough portrayal of what transpires and changes within the soul. We must embody the results of our experience with evil, and myths can do this as direct discourse cannot. In our own day we have seen a rise in the significance of indirect communication, which might mean that we are ready to let the traditional literature on sin communicate to us once again. For this to be true, for any sense of "original sin" to grip us, we must feel that men have not evolved, that we each now stand (morally) where every man has stood. If this is true, we may be in a much better position now than we have been for some years to understand the perennial problems which God faced in creation.

Chapter 12

LOVE KNOWS NO BOUNDS

On several occasions now we have discovered what seems to be an excessive action on the part of God. This does not involve irrational action, but it concerns those decisions which are either greater or less than rational norms alone might dictate. Men have intelligence at their command, but it is not perfectly distributed among us. We can control nature and sustain life, but nature is more destructive than any rational purpose might have dictated, and life is needlessly vulnerable and infested with destructive forces. God made it not impossible for us to act freely, to accept responsibility for our actions, and to do right rather than to sin, but the situation is needlessly prejudicial. In some cases the forces are stronger than man can resist or even hope to survive.

We now know ourselves to be dealing with a God who does not always take the simplest, the easiest, and the best course. Not that he does the opposite of this; it is simply that he is capable of excessive action and of electing a more dangerous course than necessary. God considered acting after the manner which Leibniz ascribed to him (i.e., creating the best of all possible worlds necessarily); but, while not completely rejecting these standards, he still elected a

146

slightly greater degree of complexity. He preferred a less obvious course than Leibniz thought he followed.

The historical record alone, we have seen, does not in itself support a more favorable outcome to this global enterprise than the partial failure—partial success—record set down to date. The world is not without individual evidences of compassion and love, but, while not totally left out, the evidence is still inconclusive that the human drama as a whole can have an ending that will reveal these to be its leading themes. To be a Christian means to have been given a sign and a promise that this is to be the case, but, on the sheer basis of present evidence, the drama does not yet appear to have a comic ending on any grand scale.

We want freedom and have been given it as available in limited quantities. Yet to be free is not absolutely required, and many will gladly reject even the opportunity to be free in order to be secure. The presence of freedom, when properly fought for and guarded, at least gives some evidence that the frame of the world was not fixed without alternative and that some changes and alterations are not inconsistent with its flexible nature as we know it. However, if any radical reconstruction is to be accomplished, it is clear that, if not impossible, it at least has not yet begun publicly. If a new "kingdom" has in fact come in spirit, it is still hard to discern much change in our outer circumstances.

Given such an in-between situation, is it also possible to believe in excessive love as characterizing God's action? Any rewriting of the final chapter into a comedy would seem to require such a belief. A cold God, or even a very proper and a just God, could simply let the drama play itself out without being in any way false to himself. The human scene gives little evidence that God feels at all bound by Kant's demand for reparations. Only a generous and an ungrudging God could be expected to do more than allow nature to take its course; this would be a divinity in whom it is possible for love to be excessive. We have observed his excessive action in other areas, so at least we can see that it is possible for him to act in this way. But do we need to go so far as to say that, if love is to be excessive, if it is to give and do more than the situation demands, and if it is intent upon others without pride of self, evil must also be as excessive as it appears to be? That is a hard statement and, if we grant God his freedom, this need not be true in some mechanical way.

If God is free not to follow the golden mean, not to thwart reason but simply not to be determined by it, if he may follow a course of greater risk and violence than needed—then at least he is also free to be excessive in other actions as well. He does not have to be excessive in evil in order to be excessive in love, and the exact limits of each need not balance perfectly. Nevertheless, his freedom to launch us on a course more strewn with suffering and destruction than he might have designed and still achieved his ends—all this at least makes excessive love a possible way in which he could act.

Whether or not he will actually do this is not an arbitrary matter, but it is flexible in its means of accomplishment for several reasons: As far as God's basic nature is concerned, he does not seem to be impulsive, and he appears to set out on a course knowing its consequences in general. He is able to support his decision in power and is never forced to abandon it. His control is sufficient to turn the tide in order to achieve his ends when he wills. He did not allow all the infinite possibles to attempt to pass into existence without imposing a certain minimum conformance to a low standard of noncontradiction, and this provides him with a situation which is not beyond control. Even granting his willingness to settle for a limited but moderately self-sustaining creation, he nevertheless is not prevented from bringing that creative effort to completion.

More than this, however, we have taken note of God's own involvement with sin. Not that he freely destroys when he does not need to, either by violence or by unkindness as men do, but he did select a world in which the odds are not as favorable for refraining from sin as they could have been. Some men are not too well equipped for the forces that play upon them and others are simply demolished by them. By not moderating the powers that play in the world more than he did and by not equipping us more democratically to meet them, God tacitly agreed to accept his share of responsibility for sin.

In that sense, he is more involved in his created order than if he had elected more favorable conditions in the first place, since his responsibility would have been fulfilled simply in the initial favorable created conditions and he could have then withdrawn to be an observer. Life and freedom and good action are not impossible in the world presented to us, but they are more difficult than they need be and are rather inequitably distributed. We can work to alter these originally not too optimum conditions, since the order is not irrevocably set along one course only. However, for the sin that is traceable to the conditions themselves, God is involved by his original choice.

In human life it is sometimes the case that we cannot love either fully or very widely or without restraint until we have first discovered our own inadequacy in some situation and admitted our own culpability to some degree. We have to tear down our self-love a little (but not completely) if self-pride is not to stand in the way of an outgoing compassion. God need not be exactly like us in this respect. Yet, if the world were a model town and community, then as men we would have little reason to expect and no ability to understand why and how God might act with excessive love and with a compassion that goes beyond its limits. It seems a rough course for God to follow when he did not need to, and even to teach us the lesson of openness does not require quite the degree of violence he imposed. Nevertheless, if we admit an excessive evil on God's part, it is at least possible for love to be excessive, and we are in a better position to understand that situation.

When men love excessively, however, it is by no means always good, just as their excessive violence is not always beneficial. Although it can be helpful, most often unrestrained affection is destructive. Excessive human love is binding and stifling; often it has the ulterior intent of making the recipient indebted and thus bound to the giver. Life is full of the destructive consequences of a love that did not keep its bounds. Excessiveness in emotion is damaging, although it is also true that Hegel and Kierkegaard are right: Nothing good in the world is accomplished without passion. If God is capable of following a course more extreme than necessary, we have to be sure that his love, which goes beyond rational bounds, is in fact a good thing. Men, of course, use love as a defensive weapon. Being insecure, they use love to gain support for themselves in insecurity. We know that God is not insecure; his chief difference from man is his infinite power which is sufficient to accomplish every aim without assistance, except that, if men will not yield, they could only be forced by being crushed and broken.

To love from an excess of power, therefore, is quite different from loving out of insecurity. Men are capable of both modes, but God only acts according to the former. His love is not beyond control, or else it could not have been restrained in the first place. It would have been more evident than it is in his plan of creation, and it would have been more clear in the order of the world just what his intentions are. God is not sentimental in his love. Compassion is not evident at every step, and it does not prevent him from using harsh forms or from employing methods more extreme than necessary. We, by way of contrast, are often helpless in our love; we become its victims in our inability to restrain it.

God stands somewhere in between these extremes. He is not sentimental in an easy and soft affection, but rather he is able to control and to restrain any tendency to immediate display. This is not a smooth path; we are not up against an easy God; he makes himself no more evident than his love. To a degree, it is better this way, but our circumstances have been pushed beyond any necessity to achieve the best effects. God can be excessive—not extreme—in releasing evil upon us. Can his love be equally excessive and still not be suffocating?

Although God need not act excessively, the extremes of destruction at least indicate his capability of moving toward an excessive action. This does not establish his love as unrestrained, but at least it allows us to see this possibility. A more friendly and a slightly better-run world might not lead us to suspect this. Love without bounds is that which also knows no depths to which it will not sink and no limits to how far it will go. The depths present in the world could have been restricted, and then life might have been less sordid. Having gone that far in allowing evil to enter in, love now also has farther to go as a result; it has more to suffer as a consequence of God's original choice.

A model world, a permanent utopia on earth, would have required God to go less far in love if he had not gone to such extremes in creation. True, he would have had to exclude some possible modes from existence, but to leave out some violence and destruction would not in itself be a bad thing to do. Some possible good modes of life were excluded in allowing some forms of evil to exist, and this is not too obviously a good way to act. We do not have evil because the fullness of creation demanded it, as Plotinus thought. Rather, even considering the need for variety and balance, what we actually have is a situation in which some good has been excluded in order to allow evil a wider range than necessary.

In the face of such a difficult situation and confronted with a God capable of acting for less than the optimum good (not willing all evil but just less good than he might have), a traditional religious attitude seems to be the only alternative to rejecting such a God. That is Job's pledge—"Though he slay me, yet will I trust in him." A happier and friendlier relationship with God might seem preferable to us, but God ruled that easy way out as unrealistic when he imposed a world upon us which is more violent than necessary. In the face of this decision, our choice is either (1) to ignore him and go our own way, or (2) to fight him and to protest that portion of his action which is unduly harsh, or else (3) to resign our own interest and not to press charges against him in spite of the evidence. Are we able to trust God when he threatens to slay us or even when he does?

Such loyalty is often demanded of us in human relations (even if it is seldom given), yet it is the hardest thing of all to remain faithful to a God who could so easily have made the path not quite so narrow and rough at little or no cost to himself. We often continue loyalty for a man even in his mistakes, because we think that, even if wrong, being what he is he cannot act otherwise. This bond of human sympathy for the person who is the victim of himself can neither be extended to God nor used to help us achieve a divine trust. For God did not have to act exactly as he did. He is not the victim of the forces in his nature but their master, even granted some basic incompatibilities which even he cannot overcome. We cannot excuse God on the same grounds that we excuse men—although for centuries theologians have tried to excuse his actions by claiming necessity for them. We often face this same situation in human relations, but it is the hardest one of all, i.e., to remain loyal when a voluntary action seems deliberately more harsh than necessary and when the perpetrator continues to protest his love.

God tries our patience more than any man could by his action in creation. God has been said to be patient with the mistakes of man, but it is not as hard for him to do this as it is for us to be patient with the world as he designed it for us. Our outrage assumes a democracy of intent on God's part, of course. If we are satisfied to accept the highest achievements and the best men, we have no problem. It is the vulgar who worry us where God is concerned. Our perplexity comes when the helpless are seen in their powerless misery and not when the successful are on view in their magnificent achievements. If God is an aristocrat, the production he has staged may be a little extravagant in its setting. It may waste too much to produce so little of quality, but an emperor has a right to enjoy spectacles at the expense of his slaves. It is only when God is said to be a democrat in his concerns that the problem becomes severe. When his actions are not completely in line with such a universal humanitarian goal, then our patience and our trust are put to a very difficult test.

Can a man relax when he is completely immersed in water?—that is the first question for us where our relationship to God is concerned. Observing God's actions in contrast with his supposed democracy of spirit and unrestricted love, a man who is sensitive to human concerns is most likely to respond violently. Our instinctive reaction is to struggle and to exert our energy in some attempted action. This is not conducive to an attitude of trust or to a condition of obedience; instead, it works against it.

There is no evidence that God intended for us to accept his conditions for the world without a fight, and he has even made it possible for us to win occasionally. But when it comes to having confidence in the excessiveness of divine love and in its ability ultimately to let nothing slip from its grasp, our given situation is more conducive to defiance than relaxation. When all is well and the sun shines, of course we can relax. When storms break out and violence reigns, then we either hide or struggle. When immersed in water, it is hard for a man to relax, particularly if the water is slightly polluted.

On the human level this does not mean that, in order to trust God, one ought not to resist evil where he can and work to make such improvements as are possible. Trust in God was never said to mean that we ought to surrender whenever other men threaten the world's peace. As the creation that God designed moves in to destroy man in the excessiveness of its use of power, then man is tested by God. However, the test demands our acceptance only of the general design; it does not require us to agree to any one alterable part without making an effort to change it.

The difficulty is that these two attitudes work against each other. A fight against the world's correctable ills makes it difficult to relax where God's ultimate intent is concerned. We react against excessive evil, and this makes it hard to trust that the love shown can be at least equally excessive. The brute presence of vast amounts of work to be done, in contrast with God's hiddenness and the non-evident nature of his future intent—all this makes it exceedingly difficult to trust in any future radical alteration of these conditions. Struggle in the present is a more natural reaction.

There is a famous Negro spiritual entitled "He's Got the Whole World in His Hands." This expresses God's claim that nothing sinks below his reach, but, given the present condition of the world, that is the hardest thing of all to believe. This difficulty is only increased when we ask why God did not take an easier and a more obvious path, since it would seem to be the only humanitarian thing to do. Both the route he chose and his means and the end announced by the Christians are not the least probable, but then neither are they the most likely divine choice which might have been predicted.

Can the less likely alternative still turn out to be true? Men act on that basis when they are feeling strong and adventuresome, but certainly it is not the safe and conservative attitude to take. Now that we have relieved God and the world from the bounds of necessity, nothing prevents the less likely from proving to be more true ultimately, but neither is this the easiest or the simplest hypothesis. Hume wants to decide important issues by majority sentiment, but evidently God's decisions are more speculative than that. At least we now are painfully aware that God does not always act in the easiest or in the least complex way, and certainly there is nothing about sophisticated scientific theory which forces us to accept the most obvious theory or to agree that things must be as they appear to be.

If we believe in the comic intent of God, i.e., that his love knows no bounds in spite of the present picture of rather widespread failure, then all we can say is this: What an incredible story and what an incredible (proposed) ending! If the less likely (not the least likely) outcome should prove true, it certainly would make a fantastic plot for a novel. Should this turn out to be the case, what does it tell us about God's nature? Why did he create as he did or why did he act (or refrain) as he did when he might have done something else?—all this tells us a great deal about his nature.

Elsewhere[31] I have tried to construct a theory of the divine nature consistent with such action, although more remains to be done. Here it is sufficient to note that a hidden and an excessive love is at least a possible answer and that we must have an incredible God as the author of an incredible story. His love may indeed know no bounds. In spite of the present appearance, he may yet have the whole world in his hands; but to relax and to trust this in the face of violence, to sustain our nerve under those conditions, is a human act that requires the strength of a God. In this case the question is whether and under what conditions he ever grants such unusual power to us or offers us the means with which to renew ourselves.

It is strange but true that ways which once led to God not only no longer do but may actually block any contemporary approach to God. Augustine and Anselm found in the hierarchical structure of the world something which led them, in steady progression, to its pinnacle and beyond that to God. We still recognize that the world is built in increasingly exclusive hierarchies, but, now that we have heard clearly about God's supposedly democratic intentions, the hierarchical order seems to lead to no God. We cannot believe that a God of love-for-all would create a world in which the obtaining of life's values is open, comparatively, to so few. John Hick believes that God will set all this aright in some eschaton; but, granted that he had various options in creation, the exclusive order with limited supply that we find ourselves locked into seems a strange way to express that purpose.

By dint of great effort we can give food and opportunity to a limited number, but even these options collapse if we do not work at them constantly. We can surmount food distribution problems, but why was it made so difficult in the first place when a minor biological and agricultural adjustment at the outset would have eliminated mass starvation? Our world is not of itself open and expansive and democratic; it is limited in supply and tightly structured and narrow in its opportunities. Within it millions starve and die needlessly. It would have taken such minor recalculations to open to everyone what we manage to hold open for so few for a limited time.

If God's love knows no bounds, the world's structure, in contrast, is surely built upon the basis of tight restrictions. We can move and we can hold doors open, but certainly not for everyone. To learn to know the world is to learn how to climb its tight and intricate hierarchies and to manipulate its pockets of power. If God is one of universal love and compassion, his design is not in keeping with his character. Any action of his at the end to open greater opportunities will never negate this fact, nor can it in any

real sense make up for his inequitable structure of creation. We must learn to understand him more on the basis
of will and emotion, or else we will fail to understand him
at all.

The world simply cannot be treated as the rational expression of a totally rational God. If his love can be seen to
be as excessive as his action in creation, we may have a
chance to discover a different God behind the world's inequitable hierarchies. The tight hierarchical structure of
the world once led aristocratically inclined men to God; to
men imbued with the spirit of democracy and freedom,
this favoritism makes God less intelligible when we realize
the more generous options which were open to him. The
restrictive bonds that limit so severely what man can do
for man seem to be overcome only by a love that exceeds
all rational demands. All that men have had to suffer, as
a result of God's choice of a more restrictive structure when
more generous provisions are available, is not, therefore,
justified. But at least we can begin to understand why God
acted in such an apparently strange manner for a democrat.

Postscript

NO MORE MYSTERY?

Have we now solved the problem of both God's nature and his action in such a way that mystery is no more? Not quite. We have asked God why he did that (i.e., selected these circumstances for creation), and, in conducting this divine interrogation, we have tried to construct a rationale for God's action. Does doing this eliminate all mystery? There are two difficulties involved in answering yes to this question: (1) the special nature of the concept of God we have arrived at, and (2) the very nature and function of concepts themselves. The only way in which we can respond for God in this interrogation is to see his action as, not out of all bounds, but as not necessitated in a precise degree.

We discover that he could have acted as he did but that no necessity drove him to it. If this is true, we are dealing with a very strong-willed God, and thus we also cannot be quite certain of our theories about him. It is possible, and perhaps even highly probable, that our theory is right; we can be sure of that. But if he did not need to act in the way he did, it is also quite possible that his motives and intentions are somewhat different than we have made them out to be.

Secondly, to have a concept of God is not the same as

159

to have God, although this is perhaps the best that man can do and something well worth having. What does it mean to have a concept of God and how does it function? A concept is a medium through which we are able to grasp and to understand existence. Everything may be "just what it is and not another thing," although actually to account for the range of nonbeing is not that simple. However, each thing is not best understood through itself alone but, rather, only through the mediation of a concept. When we use a concept, which in turn is constructed from a general theoretical framework, then the mode of existence of the object is understood if that concept is successful. As Anselm defined it, we grasp in knowledge the real existence of the object.

As it turns out, sometimes we identify the theoretical concept with the object; or sometimes, because it does possess the power of explanation, we take one effective concept to be the only possible concept. As it happens, this is not the case. A number of theoretical structures are possible and a finite variety (we know not quite how large a number) of concepts can yield an explanation and provide understanding. These all have certain similarities, and they are not radically different. Still, their flexibility is such that having one adequate concept does not in itself guarantee either that all has been explained with finality or that another concept cannot provide an acceptable alternative.

We have: (1) a mind that seeks understanding, (2) words that our minds can use, (3) concepts and their theoretical framework through which thought can grasp an object and analyze Being and nonbeing. Then, (4) we have the objects themselves, that is the infinite extent of the modes of being and nonbeing only a small portion of which are actual. Something is needed to bring such a vast range (which of itself is not internally definitely organized) into focus, and some concepts have sufficient power to accomplish this job. We can claim to have formed an adequate concept of God in this essay, although perhaps it is still in need of more elaboration. To the extent that we are successful, mystery has been removed, and this is always what a powerful and fruitful theological or scientific concept accomplishes. We end up with a framework within which we can understand God. Now we can follow the course of his action, although not with certainty, since that is not the nature of this concept or of this theoretical frame. Furthermore, the view of God constructed here depends upon an as yet unrealized and still future action, although the possibility of it is allowed for in this picture of God.

In this sense, God is understood and all mystery is removed. Were God himself a concept or if all concepts were ultimately dialectically united in only one system, as some have thought, this might be the end of the matter. However, as long as objects remain different from concepts, and as long as the modes of being and nonbeing remain not identical with the way in which they are conceived, alternative concepts will always be possible. Thought and being never achieve identity because they are two different things in spite of the fact that they are oriented to each other. To be is never identical to being conceived, in spite of Descartes's hope that this might be true. Thus, philosophy has no end, that is, as long as restless minds continue to seek an even closer avenue to Being and nonbeing.

However successful in grasping Being a concept may be —and all concepts are not equally successful—a mind is bound to realize that it still has not achieved identity with Being in its words and thoughts, and then it may restlessly move on to alter the existing concepts. Seeing that other concepts yield insight too, the sensitive mind continues in motion and refuses to rest content with the explanation it has achieved. If men lack an ability to rest within any one conceptual framework, that is, except by internal force or external suppression or lethargy, in that sense all mystery is not removed no matter how powerful the explanatory value of any given concept may be.

We began by wanting God to tell us why he acted as he did, and now what kind of an answer do we have? We have uncovered a way in which it is fully possible that God might have reasoned and acted. In just this same way, he might have used Newtonian physics as his plan in creating, but now we are not so sure that he actually did. The theory outlined above appears to fit what we know; it is not inconsistent with the world. Nevertheless, our problem is not with the world itself but with our concept about it, and it is a notorious fact that men see the world differently.

Still, this explanation fits what we know in one sense: It would not have been inconsistent or irrational for God to have acted in this way in moving to create, although we have not yet had the full range of his actions reported in order to be able to judge this with finality. However, given the flexibility that our concept visualizes as possible in God's action, he might have acted in another way too. We can assess the probabilities that he originally did and still will act according to this theory, but we cannot be certain just because we now realize that God is not bound by necessity in his own action. In that sense we have come to know God, but it is his residual uncertainty which now is the source of ours.

The mystical tradition about God is a long and very fruitful one. It should be respected in spite of our youthful impulse to have everything explained clearly once and for all. The mystical tradition matures us; it restrains a rash impulsiveness that does not ask whether its harsh demands for full explanation can possibly be satisfied or not. In order to protect God from simple judgment, a mystic impulse has often placed him above Being and thus beyond thought. According to the theory outlined here, there is an interesting sense in which he is, and yet a sense in which he is not, beyond thought.

At least in concept, we have come to understand God's nature as sharing univocal attributes with all of Being and nonbeing. In that sense, and in the sense that it is possible to form a concept about God and to give an account of his actions, God is beyond neither Being nor thought. To the extent that no concept, whatever its degree of success, is ever identical with all of Being (since it may possess only probability and not certainty)—in that real sense God remains both above the concept of Being, below nonbeing, and beyond any single thought.

Without theory, we would know neither God's nature nor the reasons for his actions nor what he might still accomplish. The particular theory offered in this essay has both the virtues and the vices of all theory. It has the virtue of allowing us to interrogate God on its terms, and then, in line with the concept we have formed, we can go on to give answers to the questions which men ask. That is no mean achievement for a theory to make possible, and it seems ungrateful of us to go farther and to demand that any theory should become either final or certain. In fact, to do so would, according to the theory given here, be a distortion of God's nature, since probability and possibility are now said to be a better clue to God than certainty and necessity.

The vice to which this theory is subject is simply that it

has the ultimate insubstantial existence of all theory, and
it can no more hold itself as identical with all of Being and
nonbeing than a concept can become the man of which it
is the concept. Through theory alone do we come to know
and to gain any insight or wield any power over Being (e.g.,
as in the physical sciences). But our elation over this important achievement must not blind us to the fact that
theories cannot by nature be one. They are more numerous
and thus more flexible than the vast modes of Being and
nonbeing which they, fortunately, are able to hold in
perspective for us.

However the world-drama turns out, someone is bound
to be surprised, since we all do not predict the same ending.
Even if this or another theory should prove to be the right
one, we may still be surprised just because every event in
fact is somehow different in occurrence from the theory
which describes it. We cling to concepts for dear life, for
they are the only medium to achieve human understanding.
We do see a few modes of Being and nonbeing directly as
objects, but our minds are still incapable of an unmediated
grasp of the vast range of all of Being and nonbeing. We
need to use tools, and theory is our shield and our means
to understand what otherwise would overwhelm our minds'
ability to absorb. Facts are too numerous for intelligibility,
and appearances are too often deceptive. Still, God's possible final action will be greater than any concept can contain, even one which is able to render it intelligible.

Christians hold on to the promise of a future which will,
by its dramatic changes, confirm God's excessive and democratic love. It is possible to understand both God and
his action to date on the basis of these encouraging words,
but it is neither easy to do so nor is it the simplest explanation. We could be mistaken; for instance, we do not

know that the statements made in the New Testament are true with certainty. In that sense mystery remains and is both unavoidable and incurable even for the Christian who believes in his promise. It is also possible that we might be wrong in the answers we have given here for God. That is the meaning of faith and why a demand of trust is both needed and not inappropriate. To say this does not require us to believe something in opposition to a reasonable solution. We have already given that, although it isn't the most reasonable explanation, since actually it outlines a more extravagant path than reason alone can account for.

Since more than one action is possible, and since the future has not yet been accomplished, these complications make any demand for certainty on our part an unreasonable request. We may trust the promise, but we do not know it to be true beyond doubt; at times of crisis and destruction, it may not even appear very likely at all. In fact, if Christians had not announced their discovery (revelation) of God's intentions, it is improbable that we would have thought of God's nature in this way merely as the result of a simple inspection of the world, not even from its better or its spiritual side. His behavior in creation actually appears more strange, rather than less, when he is depicted as an impartial democrat whose love knows no bounds. The proposed Christian solution increases the mystery and does nothing to remove it, since, if his motives are as have been described, his present actions become even harder to account for. *We remain with the mystery of a God who did not in creation, and does not always now, act immediately as he supposedly eventually intends to.*

If we look at the world and simply project back to a God capable of creating what we see, i.e., to one who is similar in nature with this world, then we will experience no inconsistency. Kierkegaard describes our difficulty over reconciling the inner and the outer man in his story about the parish priest and the regular visitor to his confessional. Because he builds up a picture of the confessor without seeing him or his actions, the priest who hears the confession experiences no inconsistency between the inner and outer nature of the speaker. Yet when we both see the world's miseries and hear extravagant promises at the same time, we are struck in the face with the discrepancy between words and facts. Which shall we accept as more true?

In human life this discrepancy is perhaps our greatest problem in understanding ourselves and the men around us, and now Christianity has created the same problem where God is concerned. If we could construct a concept of God by simply observing his overt action, this would cause us no problem at all, because all we would need to do is to describe his actions in a manner consistent with our theory. When Christians tell us what they have experienced God's nature to be like and what they have discovered his intentions for the future to be, this solves no rational problems. It only increases the difficulty because we experience, in an extreme form, a harsh contrast between words of promise and present action whenever the Christian God is placed alongside the world as it is. This seems to indicate that we could not have guessed, as the most reasonable alternative, that God's nature is capable of such excessive love, that is, if Christians had not first suggested it as a result of their spiritual transformation.

The world has its impersonal and its horrifying aspects, so that, even if we accept the Christian picture, we cannot take it simply as it presents itself. We must construct a view of God which also accounts for why we did not think of him in this way before simply as a result of our natural, physical observations. Any acceptable view of a Christian God must account for why it is so difficult to believe that he is as he has been announced to be and why such belief is so severe a test of our trust—like trying to relax while being immersed in the waters of a raging flood. Who has the power to still such troubled waters? Where is the spiritual life that is stronger and more enduring than this fascinating and terrifyingly solid physical world?

NOTES

1. The chapters that follow are an attempt to open the issues to a new perspective; they are not intended to review either the past or the present literature on the subject. However, the reader may be particularly interested to compare:

Bourke, Vernon, *Will in Western Thought* (Sheed & Ward, Inc., 1964).

Buber, Martin, *Good and Evil: Two Interpretations,* tr. by Ronald Gregor Smith and Michael Bullock (Charles Scribner's Sons, 1953).

Camus, Albert, *The Rebel,* tr. by Anthony Bower (Random House, Inc., Vintage Books, 1956).

Farrer, Austin, *Love Almighty and Ills Unlimited* (Doubleday & Company, Inc., 1961).

Ferré, Nels F. S., *Evil and the Christian Faith* (Harper and Brothers, 1947).

Hick, John, *Evil and the God of Love* (London: Macmillan & Co., Ltd., 1966).

Kerenyi, Carl, *et al., Evil: Studies in Jungian Thought* (Northwestern University Press, 1967).

Ricoeur, Paul, *The Symbolism of Evil,* tr. by Emerson Buchanan (Harper & Row, Publishers, Inc., 1967).

Sartre, Jean-Paul, *The Devil and the Good Lord,* tr. by Kitty Black (Alfred A. Knopf, Inc., 1960).

Simon, Ulrich, *A Theology of Auschwitz* (London: Victor Gollancz, Ltd., 1967).

Siwek, Paul, *The Philosophy of Evil* (The Ronald Press, 1951).

2. For a review of this kind, see particularly John Hick, *Evil and the God of Love.*

3. See my *Divine Perfection: Possible Ideas of God* (Harper & Brothers, 1962; also published in the Library of Philosophy and Theology, SCM Press, Ltd., London, 1962).

4. For a discussion of the empirical base for thought about God, see my *The Existentialist Prolegomena: To a Future Metaphysics* (The University of Chicago Press, 1969).

5. My work entitled *The God of Evil: An Argument from the Existence of the Devil* (Harper & Row, Publishers, Inc., 1970).

6. I am attempting to do this in a work as yet unpublished.

7. For one aspect of this orientation, see my *The Future of Theology* (The Westminster Press, 1969).

8. See Plato, *The Republic,* tr. by F. M. Cornford (Oxford University Press, 1945), p. 71.

9. Leibniz, *Theodicy,* tr. by E. M. Huggard (Yale University Press, 1952).

10. David Hume, *Dialogues Concerning Natural Religion,* ed. by Norman K. Smith (The Bobbs-Merrill Company, Inc., 1947).

11. Leibniz, *Theodicy.*

12. C. G. Jung, *Answer to Job,* tr. by R. F. C. Hull (Meridian Books, 1960).

13. Anselm, *Cur Deus Homo,* in *St. Anselm: Basic*

Writings, tr. by S. N. Deane (Open Court Publishing Co., 1962).

14. Søren Kierkegaard, *Fear and Trembling,* tr. by Walter Lowrie (Princeton University Press, 1945).

15. See Carl Kerenyi, *et al., Evil: Studies in Jungian Thought* (Northwestern University Press, 1967). All page references in this section are to this volume.

16. J. R. R. Tolkien, *The Lord of the Rings,* 3 vols. (Ballantine Books, 1965).

17. *Plato and Parmenides,* tr. by F. N. Cornford (London: Routledge and Kegan Paul, Ltd., 1958).

18. Leibniz, *Theodicy.*

19. For a detailed account of how this can be done, see my *The God of Evil.*

20. Paul Ricoeur, *The Symbolism of Evil.*

21. Søren Kierkegaard, *Either/Or,* tr. by D. F. and L. M. Swenson (London: Oxford University Press, 1944), Vol. I, pp. 179–188.

22. Friedrich Nietzsche, *Beyond Good and Evil,* tr. by Marianne Cowan (Henry Regnery Co., Gateway Edition, 1955).

23. For a "process" treatment of the problem of evil in the story of Job, see, for example, Charles Hartshorne, *A Natural Theology for Our Time* (Open Court Publishing Co., 1967), pp. 116 ff.

24. John Hick, *Evil and the God of Love.*

25. Sigmund Freud, *The Future of an Illusion,* tr. by W. D. Robinson-Scott (Doubleday Anchor Books, 1957). All page references in this section are to this volume.

26. Spinoza, *Ethics,* ed. by James Gutmann (Hafner Publishing Co., 1960), Appendix to Book I, p. 75.

27. Albert Camus, *The Rebel,* p. 23.

28. Jean-Paul Sartre, *The Devil and the Good Lord,* tr.

by Kitty Black (Random House, Inc., Vintage Books, 1962), p. 141.

29. Søren Kierkegaard, *The Concept of Dread,* tr. by Walter Lowrie (Princeton University Press, 1946).

30. Martin Buber, *Good and Evil.*

31. In my book *The God of Evil.*